18.00

114066

D1341444

Friedrich Kiesler
Designer

SITZMÖBEL DER 30ER UND 40ER JAHRE
SEATING FURNITURE OF THE 30S AND 40S

ÖSTERREICHISCHE FRIEDRICH UND LILLIAN KIESLER-PRIVATSTIFTUNG
AUSTRIAN FREDERICK AND LILLIAN KIESLER PRIVATE FOUNDATION

HATJE CANTZ

Inhalt Contents

Vorwort

Um den Gegenstand, der ästhetisch erlebt werden will, erfahrbar zu machen, muss er nachgeschaffen, seine Idee im Geiste nachgebildet werden. Dies stellt der Kunsthistoriker Erwin Panofsky 1940 fest und beschreibt damit das Bemühen der Geisteswissenschaften, die Bedeutung von Kunstwerken zu erfassen. Es sind „menschliche Zeugnisse, die aus dem Strom der Zeit auftauchen" und auf ihre Absichten hin befragt werden. In diesem Sinne widmet sich auch die Kiesler Stiftung dem architektonischen, künstlerischen und theoretischen Werk Friedrich Kieslers. Den in Wien beheimateten Nachlass des austro-amerikanischen Künstlers zu bearbeiten und Impuls gebend in den zeitgenössischen Diskurs einzubinden, ist Aufgabe und Ziel dieser Forschungsinstitution. Bereits 1997 schloss sich Wittmann diesem Interesse an Kieslers Schaffen an und ermöglichte, mit der Hilfe weiterer privater Gönner, den Erwerb der umfassenden Bestände von Kieslers Witwe und zweiter Frau Lillian durch die Republik Österreich und die Stadt Wien.

Das gemeinsame Interesse an Kieslers Theorie zur *Design Correlation* und seinem wohl berühmtesten Designobjekt, dem *Correalistischen Möbel*, gaben vor mehr als zwei Jahren den Ausschlag, gemeinsam den künstlerischen Absichten des Designers nachzugehen und auf wissenschaftlicher Grundlage den Nachbau der Möbel zu forcieren. Ein wesentliches Ergebnis dieser Kooperation ist die vorliegende Publikation, die erstmals einen Überblick über Kieslers Sitzmöbeldesign von den ersten Skizzen der 20er bis hin zu den Entwürfen der späten 40er Jahre des 20. Jahrhunderts liefert und bisher unbekannte Aspekte von Kieslers künstlerischer Entwicklung beleuchtet.

Die geisteswissenschaftliche Erforschung von Kieslers Entwürfen erfährt im praktischen Nachvollzug, in der Re-Edition, eine Erfüllung, wie sie eine theoretische Auseinandersetzung allein nicht leisten kann. Die enge Zusammenarbeit der beiden Unternehmen folgt damit auch der nachdrücklichen Forderung von Kiesler, sich vor allem am Wohlbefinden des Menschen zu orientieren und die herkömmliche Funktionalität eines gestalteten Objektes, einer Couch, eines Sessels, eines Bettes zu überdenken – über das Tradierte hinauszugehen. Mit dem *Correalistischen Möbel*, der *Party Lounge* und *Bed Couch* stehen uns heute wieder variable und vielseitig einsetzbare Objekte zur Verfügung. Ihre Wandlungsfähigkeit veranschaulicht deutlich die künstlerische Absicht, ein flexibles und gleichermaßen ästhetisches Erleben im Gebrauch des Gegenstandes sichtbar zu machen. Friedrich Kieslers Werk, so wie es auf uns gekommen ist, begegnete uns bislang vor allem im musealen Kontext. In der Re-Edition jedoch werden seine Ideen als integrative Bestandteile unseres Alltags nutzbar gemacht.

Dieter Bogner

Kiesler Stiftung Wien

Heinz F. Hofer-Wittmann

Wittmann Möbelwerkstätten

Preface

In order to permit us to experience the object aesthetically, it is necessary to re-create it, to reproduce its idea in our mind. This was observed by the art historian Erwin Panofsky in 1940, thus describing the endeavor of the humanities to apprehend the meaning of art works. These are "human testimonies that surface from the river of time" and which are questioned in terms of their intentions. In this spirit, the Kiesler Foundation also focuses on the architectural, artistic and theoretical work of Frederick Kiesler. The task and mission of this research institution is to process the estate of the Austro-American artist, that is kept in Vienna, and to incorporate it as fresh impetus into the contemporary discourse. As early as 1997, Wittmann took up this interest in Kiesler's work and, with the aid of a few other private benefactors, enabled the Republic of Austria and the City of Vienna to acquire the extensive material from Kiesler's widow and second wife Lillian.

A shared interest in Kiesler's theory of *Design Correlation* and what is probably his most famous design object, the *Correalist Furniture*, were the driving force behind the decision taken more than two years ago jointly to explore the designer's artistic intentions and to promote the reconstruction of his furniture on a scientific basis. This publication is one important result of this co-operation, providing the first overview of Kiesler's seat furniture design, from his first sketches from the nineteen-twenties, to his designs of the late forties, and highlighting as yet unknown aspects of the Kiesler's artistic development.

Practical reconstruction of Kiesler's designs in the re-edition fulfils the goal of human-research in such a way that a theoretical exploration alone cannot accomplish. The close co-operation of both organisations is hence equally in keeping with Kiesler's emphatic call to orient design above all to human well-being, and to reconsider the conventional functionality of a designed object, a couch, a chair, a bed – and to go beyond traditions. Today, once again, the *Correalist Furniture*, the *Party Lounge*, and *Bed Couch* are available to us as variable and multifunctional objects. Their flexibility clearly illustrates the artistic intention of visualizing a flexible and at the same time aesthetic experience in using the object. Previously, Frederick Kiesler's work, as it has come down to us, was found above all in a museum setting. In the re-edition, in contrast, his ideas are harnessed as integral components of our everyday life.

Dieter Bogner

Kiesler Foundation Vienna

Heinz F. Hofer-Wittmann

Wittmann Möbelwerkstätten

Einleitung

Eine *Re-Edition* bedeutet die Wiederaufnahme vergangener Äußerungen eines künstlerischen Ausdrucks. Der historische Fakt aus dem überlieferten Bestand ist der geschichtswissenschaftlichen Kategorisierung längst anvertraut, ja einverleibt und erfährt jetzt eine Neubewertung der besonderen Art. Der Bedeutungsgewinn, der diesem Werk so lange Zeit nach seinem Entstehen nun beigemessen wird, ist mit seiner *Aktualität* im Hier und Jetzt begründet. Kaum etwas ehrt so sehr, vor allem die Kunst und das Design, wie der Status unmittelbarer Gegenwärtigkeit. Das so Ausgezeichnete kann also seit seinem Bestehen zumindest auf zwei Phasen von hoher zeitgenössischer Akzeptanz verweisen. Erstere liegt in der Vergangenheit und war von einer Qualität, die ein Überdauern wahrscheinlich erst möglich machte. Die zweite Phase ist von *Wiederbelebung* gekennzeichnet, ist Teil unserer Gegenwart und nimmt allein schon deshalb unsere Aufmerksamkeit in Anspruch, verlangt zumindest nach ihr – wie auch andere Äußerungen *unserer Zeit*.

Für den Designer, Architekten und Künstler Friedrich Kiesler steht seit den 20er Jahren ein sich wandelndes, sehr anpassungsfähiges kreatives Schaffen im Mittelpunkt des künstlerischen Interesses. In seinen Theorien und Konzepten spürt Kiesler den Bedürfnissen seiner Zeit und ihrer Menschen nach, um diese dann als Gestalt gebende Faktoren in sein Werk einfließen zu lassen. Es sind nicht nur die neuesten technologischen Standards und naturwissenschaftlichen Erkenntnisse, die seine Auseinandersetzung prägen, auch die geistigen Dispositionen – psychologische, soziologische und philosophische Komponenten – formen Kieslers universales Weltenmodell. Die sehr Praxis bezogenen Überlegungen in seiner Theorie des *Correalismus* richten sich dabei vorwiegend auf das sogenannte *technological environment* – auf die vom Menschen gestaltete Umwelt, auf die Gesetzmäßigkeiten einander bedingender Kräfte und Strukturen. Kiesler fordert für jede Art der Einwirkung d. h. Gestaltung unserer Umwelt die entsprechenden Maßnahmen der Überprüfung von Funktion und Wirkung der angewandten Formen und Mittel, sowie die Anpassung an den aktuellen Stand der Anforderungen. So orientiert er sich schon Ende der 20er Jahre an der „modernen Massenzivilisation bzw. Massenkultur, sowie dem ihr innewohnenden Geschwindigkeitskult", macht die Wahl der Materialien (Holz, Glas, Metall) von ihrer psychofunktionalen Entsprechung abhängig und konstruiert die Form des Gegenstandes nach seinem Zweck und Nutzen. Mit dem Begriff *tool* (Instrument, Werkzeug) definiert Kiesler jenes verbindende Element, das seine universale Wirklichkeitsauffassung mit seinen praktischen Vorstellungen verknüpft. Unter *tool* versteht er jede Art von Ergänzung, die vom Menschen gemacht oder erdacht wird: „In diesem Sinne ist alles, von dem der Mensch in seinem Existenzkampf Gebrauch macht, ein *tool* (...) vom Hemd zum Unterstand, von der Kanone bis zur Dichtung, vom Telefon bis zur Malerei."[1]

Kiesler überprüft seine Thesen vorwiegend anhand des künstlerischen Designs – Ziel seiner Bestrebungen ist es, das auf alle Sinne wirkende *tool* mit „den Mitteln und dem Ausdruck unserer Epoche" im kontinuierlichen Ineinandergreifen von Architektur, Skulptur und Malerei darzulegen. Seine Ambition künstlerische

8

---

1   Frederick Kiesler, „On Correalism and Biotechnique. A Definition and Test of a New Approach to Building Design",
     in: *Architectural Record*, September 1939, S. 63. (Orig. Zit. in Engl.)

Introduction

A *Re-edition* implies the resumption of past manifestations of an artistic expression. The historical fact from the original work that has come down to us has long since been categorized – indeed assimilated – by historical science, and is now being reappraised in a special way. The gain in meaning, that is now being attached to this work so many years after its creation, is justified by its *topical relevance* in the here and now. Nothing is quite as flattering, above all in art and design, as the status of immediate presence. That which is distinguished thus boasts at least two phases of great contemporary acceptance since it came into existence. The first lies in the past, and was of such quality that probably ensured that it would stand the test of time. The second phase is characterized by *revival*, is part of our present and, ipso facto, draws – at least demands – our attention like many other statements of our time.

For the designer, architect and artist Frederick Kiesler, the focus of artistic interest was on a changing, highly adaptable creativity since the nineteen-twenties. In his theories and concepts, Kiesler investigates the needs of his time and of the people, so as to incorporate them into his work as form-giving factors. It is not only the latest technological standards and findings of natural science that characterize his analysis, but equally so the intellectual dispositions – psychological, sociological and philosophical components – that shape Kiesler's universal world-model. The very practical considerations in his theory of *Correalism* are geared primarily to the *technological environment*, as he called it – to the man-made environment, to the laws of mutually conditional forces and structures. For each type of influence, i. e. shaping of our environment, Kiesler demands appropriate measures of reviewing the function and effect of the applied forms and means, as well as adaptation thereof to the current status of requirements. Accordingly, he already orientated himself by "modern mass civilization and mass culture and their inherent cult of speed" at the end of the twenties, making his choice of materials (wood, glass, metal) dependent on their psycho-functional effect, and designing the form of the object according to its purpose and practical use. Kiesler uses the term *tool* to define the connecting element that joins his universal conception of reality with his practical ideas. To him, *tool* implies any kind of addition made or devised by man: "In this sense everything which man uses in his struggle for existence is a tool (…) from shirts to shelter, from cannons to poetry, from telephones to painting."[1]

Kiesler verifies his theories primarily on the basis of artistic design – the aim of his efforts is to expound the *tool*, acting on all of our senses, with "the means and the expression of our age" in the continuous intermeshing of architecture, sculpture and painting. His ambition to marry fields of artistic activity, and to comprehend creative work as a form of technology lends topical importance to Kiesler's conception of the work and justifies its re-integration into the discourse on current design. This programmatic adherence to the intimate inter-

9

1   Frederick Kiesler, "On Correalism and Biotechnique. A Definition and Test of a New Approach to Building Design", in: *Architectural Record,* September 1939, p. 63.

Wirkungsfelder miteinander zu verschmelzen, sowie das kreative Schaffen als eine Form der Technologie zu begreifen – verleiht Kieslers Werkidee Aktualität und legitimiert ihre erneute Einbindung in den Diskurs über aktuelles Design. Das programmatische Festhalten an der engen Wechselbeziehung von Funktion und Form im künstlerischen Gestalten, welches letztendlich seine Abkehr vom Internationalen Stil einleitete, zeichnet sich auch in seinen *bewegten* Entwürfen zum *Correalistischen Instrument* von 1942 ab. Wenige Jahre später liefert uns die biomorphe Formgebung von Kieslers *Endless House* die Entsprechung einer von den Kräften des Lebens gestalteten Wohneinheit. In seinem Artikel *Pseudo Functionalism in Modern Architecture* betont Kiesler 1949 noch einmal, dass – im Gegensatz zu Louis Sullivans Motto: „Form folgt der Funktion" – die Form nicht der Funktion folgt, sondern: "(…) Die Funktion folgt der Vision. Die Vision folgt der Realität."[2]

Die Re-Edition von Friedrich Kieslers *Correalistischen Möbeln*, der *Party Lounge* und *Bed Couch* ruft uns demnach nicht nur ein Formenrepertoire in Erinnerung, das aufgrund modischer Entwicklungen mit Anerkennung rechnen darf. Vielmehr sind es die künstlerischen Intentionen einer zweckgebundenen Flexibilität und der daraus abgeleiteten Form, die *unserer Zeit* zu einer vorbildhaften Ästhetik verhilft. Denn unsere unmittelbare Wirklichkeit verlangt auch heute nach einer *Kunst-Realität*, die aus dem Beziehungsgeflecht der verschiedenen Lebenskomponenten erwächst. Untrennbar mit dem Fluss des täglichen Lebens verknüpft mündet sie in Kreationen, die Traum und Wirklichkeit miteinander verschmelzen lassen.

Monika Pessler

Kiesler Stiftung Wien

2   Frederick Kiesler, „Pseudo Functionalism in Modern Architecture", in: *Partisan Review*, Juli 1949, S. 733-742.

play of function and form in artistic design, which was ultimately to lead to his renunciation of the International Style, is also to be observed in his *moving* plans for the *Correalist Instrument* of 1942. A few years later, the biomorphic design of Kiesler's *Endless House* was the translation of this concept into a living unit shaped by the forces of life. In his article *Pseudo-Functionalism in Modern Architecture* Kiesler emphasized once again in 1949 that, in contrast to Louis Sullivan's motto: "Form follows function" – form does not follow function but rather that "(…) Function follows vision. Vision follows reality".[2]

The re-edition of Frederick Kiesler's *Correalist Furniture*, the *Party Lounge* and *Bed Couch*, therefore not only recalls to mind a repertory of forms that can expect to receive recognition in view of fashionable trends. Rather, it is the artistic intentions of a purpose-bound flexibility and the form derived from it that helps our time achieve an exemplary aesthetic. For today too, our immediate reality demands an *art-reality* that evolves from the mesh of correlations between various components of life. Inseparably linked with the flow of everyday life, it leads to creations that blend dream and reality.

Monika Pessler

Kiesler Foundation Vienna

2   Frederick Kiesler, "Pseudo Functionalism in Modern Architecture", in: *Partisan Review,* July 1949, pp. 733-742.

1   Friedrich Kiesler bei der Ankunft in New York 1926.

Foto: Underwood & Underwood.

Frederick Kiesler arriving in New York in 1926.

Photograph by Underwood & Underwood.

Sitzmöbel als Architektur
Seat Furniture as Architecture

13

Harald Krejci

1

Sitzmöbel als Architektur

Der 1890 in Czernowitz geborene Architekt Friedrich Kiesler beginnt seine künstlerische Laufbahn im Wien der frühen 20er Jahre. Er realisiert die Wiener *Raumbühne* und die Gestaltung der „Internationalen Ausstellung neuer Theatertechnik" 1924, (Abb. 2, 3) ehe er mit der *Raumstadt* 1925 (Abb. 4) erfolgreich in den Kreis der europäischen Künstler-Avantgarde aufgenommen wird. Friedrich Kiesler findet dort als letztes offizielles Mitglied der holländischen Avantgarde-Gruppe De Stijl geistige Mitstreiter für seine kompromisslosen Ansätze einer dynamischen Raumauffassung und seiner damit verbundenen universalen Gestalttheorie. Der Maler und Theoretiker Theo van Doesburg ist ein großer Befürworter von Kieslers Architekturkonzept und schreibt euphorisch über die Ausstellungsgestaltungen: „In keiner Stadt der Welt habe ich etwas Ähnliches gesehen. [...] bei dieser Art der Demonstration wurden die engsten Beziehungen zwischen den verschiedenen Arbeiten durch ihre Anordnung im Raum erzielt",[1] und konstatiert: „Du hast das getan was wir alle hofften eines Tages zu tun. Das ist die Vereinigung der Künste."[2] Ausstellungsmöbel und Architekturmodell in einem, diese Erweiterung des Gegenstandes in seiner funktionalen Bedeutung bildet einen der wichtigen gestalterischen Grundsätze Friedrich Kieslers. Er entspringt einer ganzheitlichen Raumauffassung, die in der Folge auch seine Möbelentwürfe beeinflusst. Über die erweiterte Funktion des Möbels resümiert Kiesler 1947: „Die verschiedenen Funktionen waren in den grundlegenden Strukturen der ursprünglichen Zelle enthalten, genauso wie die vielfältigen, spezialisierten Funktionen von Organen bereits im amorphen Embryo des menschlichen Körpers enthalten sind."[3] Der menschliche Körper ist daher nicht nur gestalterische Metapher für die Form, sondern liefert in der Komplexität der Funktionszusammenhänge eine Möglichkeit, das Potenzial einer multifunktionalen Objekterfassung auszuloten, welche sich ganz nach den menschlichen Bedürfnissen richtet.

Exposition des Arts Décoratifs et Industriels Modernes

Ein wichtiges Ereignis sowohl in der Designgeschichte als auch für Friedrich Kieslers Möbeldesign bildet die 1925 stattfindende Kunstgewerbeschau „Exposition des Arts Décoratifs et Industriels Modernes" in Paris. Der Mitbegründer der Wiener Secession und der Wiener Werkstätten Josef Hoffmann beauftragt Kiesler mit der Gestaltung der Theatersektion des Österreichischen Pavillons. Die sogenannte *Raumstadt* Kieslers erweist sich im Kreis der Avantgarde Künstler als großer Erfolg. Die anderen Pavillons der Gewerbeschau werden den in sie gesetzten Erwartungen nicht gerecht, wie auch die Gesamtschau ihr proklamiertes Ziel – Modelle und Werke neuer Inspiration oder wirklicher Originalität zu umfassen und Kopien, Imitationen oder Nachahmungen alter Stile auszuschließen –, nicht erreicht.[4] Die Verantwortlichen orientieren sich in ihrer Auswahl an den abstraktornamentalen Objekten der Wiener Werkstätte oder den französischen Vertretern

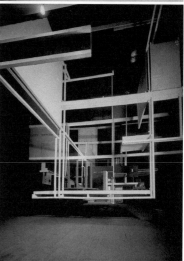

1   Frederick Kiesler, „New Display Techniques for ‚Art of This Century' designed by Frederick Kiesler", in: *Architectural Forum,* 78, 2, 1943, S. 50.
2   Thomas H. Creighton, „Kiesler's Pursuit of an Idea", in: *Progressive Architecture,* 42, 7, 1961, S. 104.
3   Frederick Kiesler, „Manifest du Corréalisme", in: *L'Architecture d'Aujourd'hui,* 6, 1949, S. 145.
4   Heinz Hirdina, „Die Avantgarde und der Weg nach Byzanz", in: *Form + Zweck,* 9+10, 1994, S. 81 ff.

Seat Furniture as Architecture

The architect Frederick Kiesler, born in Cernauti in 1890, began his artistic career in Vienna in the early nineteen-twenties. He created the Vienna *Space Stage* and designed the "International Exhibition of New Theatre Technique" in 1924, (Fig. 2, 3) before successfully joining the ranks of the European artist avant-garde with *City in Space* (Fig. 4) in 1925. As the last official member of the Dutch avant-garde group De Stijl, it is there that Frederick Kiesler found intellect support for his uncompromising approaches to a dynamic conception of space and his associated universal design theory. The painter and theorist Theo van Doesburg was a great believer in Kiesler's concept of architecture and wrote euphorically of his exhibition designs, "In no city in the world have I seen anything similar to it. [...] in this method of demonstration the closest relations between the different works were established by their arrangement in space."[1] and notes, "You have done what we all hoped to accomplish one day. To unite the arts."[2] Exhibition furniture and architectural model in one, this extension of the object in its functional significance constitutes one of Frederick Kiesler's key design principles. It is born of a holistic conception of space that was subsequently also to impact on his furniture designs. Regarding the extended function of furniture, Kiesler summarized his understanding as follows in 1947, "The different functions were contained in the primary structure of the initial cell just as the multiple, specialized functions of organs are already contained in the amorphous embryo of the human body."[3] The human body is hence not only a design-based metaphor of form, but, in the complexity of its functional relations, also provides a possibility of gauging the potential of a multifunctional perception of the object that is strongly geared to human needs.

Exposition des Arts Décoratifs et Industriels Modernes

15

A major event both in the history of design and for Frederick Kiesler's furniture design was the arts and crafts show "Exposition des Arts Décoratifs et Industriels Modernes" held in Paris in 1925. Co-founder of the Vienna Secession and the Wiener Werkstätten (Vienna Workshops) Josef Hoffmann commissioned Kiesler to design the theatre section of the Austrian pavilion. Kiesler's *Raumstadt*, as he called it, proved to be a major success among the avant-garde artists. The other pavilions at the arts show failed to come up to expectations, just as the overall show failed to achieve its declared goal – to showcase models and works of new inspiration and real originality and to disregard copies or imitations of previous styles.[4] The organizers based their selection on the abstract, ornamental objects of the Wiener Werkstätten or the French exponents of Art Nouveau and Art Déco. Dominated by traditional craft work, the show remained committed to a luxury-ridden, ornamental, labored use of forms. The pavilion by Émile-Jacques Ruhlmann or interior designs by

1   Frederick Kiesler, "New Display Techniques for 'Art of This Century' designed by Frederick Kiesler",
     in: *Architectural Forum*, 78, 2, 1943, p. 50.
2   Thomas H. Creighton, "Kiesler's Pursuit of an Idea", in: *Progressive Architecture*, 42, 7, 1961, p. 104.
3   Frederick Kiesler, "Manifest du Corréalisme", in: *L'Architecture d'Aujourd'hui*, 6, 1949, p. 145.
4   Heinz Hirdina, "Die Avantgarde und der Weg nach Byzanz", in: *Form + Zweck*, 9+10, 1994, p. 81 ff.

des Jugendstils und des Art Déco. Dominiert von traditionell ausgerichtetem Kunsthandwerk bleibt die Schau einer luxuriös behafteten, ornamentalen, schwerfälligen Formensprache verpflichtet. Der Pavillon von Émile-Jacques Ruhlmann oder Interieurs von André Groult deuten einen opulenten Lebensstil an und demonstrieren die Vorherrschaft französischen Handwerks. (Abb. 6-8) Deutschland hätte beispielsweise mit seinen neuesten Designentwürfen, – etwa den Stahlrohrmöbeln von Marcel Breuer –, einen wichtigen Beitrag leisten können, wurde jedoch nicht zur Ausstellung eingeladen.[5] Einigen wenigen Architekten gelingt es dennoch, Baustil und Möbelentwürfe der Moderne auf der Schau zu präsentieren, darunter Le Corbusier, der ohne finanzielle Unterstützung und mit zeitlicher Verzögerung den Pavillon *L'Esprit Nouveau* realisiert.[6] (Abb. 9)

Amerikanische Künstler und Architekten sind auf der Gewerbeschau in Paris nicht vertreten. Diese Verweigerung liegt im Gutachten einer Expertenkommission begründet, die im Vorfeld feststellte, dass in Amerika kein modernes Design produziert würde. Die Möglichkeit der lukrativen Vermarktung französischer Art Déco-Möbel stößt bei den amerikanischen Händlern jedoch auf großes Interesse. Vertreter von über 100 Handelsorganisationen und Kunstverbänden unterstreichen in ihrem Bericht die beispielgebende Rolle dieser Ausstellung und empfehlen der amerikanischen Industrie die Errichtung und Institutionalisierung modernen Designs in Amerika.[7] Kiesler veröffentlicht im Juli 1925 in *Der Querschnitt*[8] eine Reportage zur Ausstellung, in der er die konsequente Schlichtheit in Form und Material des Russischen und Dänischen Pavillons lobt. Seine Kritik richtet sich gegen die unmotiviert kitschig anmutenden Bauten, sowie gegen die unzeitgemäße, romantisierende Vorstellung einer kunsthandwerklichen Güterproduktion: „An der gesamten Ausstellung [...] erhärtet sich der Protest der internationalen Avantgarde der Künstler und des Publikums gegen das Kunstgewerbe. [...] Sie [die Ausstellung] beweist völlig überzeugend die Überflüssigkeit eines Gewerbes, dessen Endziel expressionistische Lafetten sind."[9] Über die möglichen Auswirkungen dieser Ausstellung auf die Situation in Amerika schreibt Kiesler polemisch: „Amerika, das keine Kunstgewerbeindustrie besitzt und daher in der glücklichen Lage war, sich an dieser Ausstellung nicht beteiligen zu können, wird [...] erfahren, dass [...] [es] zur Rettung der Nation mit der Nachahmung europäischen Kunstgewerbes zu beginnen habe."[10] Kieslers Befürchtung, dass diese Kunstgewerbeschau eine falsche Interpretation von zeitgemäßem Design in Amerika provozieren könnte, sollte sich in den folgenden Jahren teilweise bewahrheiten.

Im Januar 1926 verlässt Kiesler mit seiner Frau Steffi Paris mit dem Ziel, in New York einen von Jane Heap vermittelten Auftrag für eine Ausstellung über europäische Theatertechnik, sowie den Bau seines *Endless Theater* realisieren zu können. Vor allem ökonomische Gründe mögen Kiesler zu diesem Schritt in eine ungewisse Zukunft bewogen haben. Die wirtschaftliche Situation in Europa zu jener Zeit ist

5   Ebd.
6   Le Corbusier erwähnt in einem Brief an Vaneck: „Unzählige Pavillons werden errichtet, alle werden dekoriert und wirken dekorativ und das ist wirklich ein Spektakel welches einem den Eindruck totaler Verrücktheit gibt. Ich dachte nicht, dass das Niveau so niedrig ist". Zitiert nach Carol S. Eliel, *L'Esprit Nouveau, Purism in Paris* 1918-1925, New York 2001, S. 49.
7   Hirdina 1994 (wie Anm. 4).
8   Friedrich Kiesler, „Ménagerie des Arts Decoratifs et Industriels Modernes Paris 1925", in: *Der Querschnitt*, 5, 7 1925, S. 609-612.
9   Ebd. S. 609.
10   Ebd. S. 612.

André Groult suggested an opulent life-style and demonstrated the predominance of French craft. (Fig. 6-8) Germany, for example, could have made an important contribution with its latest designs, such as Marcel Breuer's steel tube furniture, but was not invited to the exhibition.[5] A few architects still succeeded in presenting modern building styles and furniture designs at the show, including Le Corbusier, who installed the pavilion L'Esprit Nouveau without any financial support and with some delay.[6] (Fig. 9)

No American artists or architects featured at the art show in Paris. This refusal was due to an expertise drawn up by a commission of experts in the run-up to the show who observed that America did not produce any modern design. However, American dealers were extremely interested in the possibility of marketing French Art Déco furniture for good profit. In their report, representatives of more than one hundred trade organizations and art associations underscored the exemplary role of this exhibition and recommended that the American industry establish and institutionalize modern design in America.[7] In July 1925, Kiesler published a report on the exhibition in Der Querschnitt,[8] in which he praised the rigorous simplicity of form and material of the Russian and Danish pavilion. His criticism was of pointlessly kitschy buildings and of the old-fashioned, romanticizing idea of craft production: "The overall exhibition […] substantiates the protest of the international avant-garde of artists and the public against arts and crafts. […] It [the exhibition] proves absolutely conclusively the superfluousness of a craft whose ultimate goal is to create expressionist mounts."[9] Regarding the possible effects of this exhibition on the situation in America, Kiesler writes polemically, "America, that has no craft industry and therefore was in the fortunate position not to be able to participate in this exhibition, will […] realize that […] [it] will have to begin imitating European crafts in order to save the nation."[10] Kiesler's fear that this art show could provoke a misinterpretation of contemporary design in America was to be confirmed to some extent in the following years.

In January 1926, Kiesler left Paris with his wife Steffi to carry out a contract arranged by Jane Heap for an exhibition on European theatre techniques in New York, and to build his Endless Theater. Financial reasons may have been foremost in inducing Kiesler to take this step into an uncertain future. The economic situation in Europe at the time was characterized by the repercussions of World War I. The restricted building activity made it hard for architects to establish a livelihood in Austria. America, in contrast, was enjoying a fifty-percent increase in building contracts for roads and residential houses. In addition, numerous tower blocks and bridges were being built in New York. Technical consumer products such as radios and cars were also increasingly

5   Op. cit.
6   In a letter to Vaneck, Le Corbusier mentions, "Countless pavilions are being built, all of them are being decorated and look decorative, and that is really a spectacle that creates the impression of total madness. I did not think that the standards were so low." Quoted after Carol S. Eliel, L'Esprit Nouveau, Purism in Paris 1918-1925, New York 2001, p. 49.
7   Hirdina 1994 (cf. note 4).
8   Friedrich Kiesler, "Ménagerie des Arts Decoratifs et Industriels Modernes Paris 1925", in: Der Querschnitt, 5, 7 1925, p. 609-612. (Orig. quot. in Ger.)
9   Op. cit. p. 609.
10 Op. cit. p. 612.

geprägt von den Auswirkungen des 1. Weltkriegs. Die nun eingeschränkte Bautätigkeit macht es für Architekten schwer, sich in Österreich eine Existenzgrundlage zu schaffen. Amerika hingegen erlebt eine 50-prozentige Steigerung der Bauaufträge im Straßen- und Einfamilienhausbau. Zudem entstehen in New York zahlreiche Hochhäuser und Brücken. Technische Konsumgüter, wie Radios und Autos finden ebenfalls immer stärkeren Absatz. Vielleicht spekuliert Kiesler mit seinem Umzug nach New York auf weitere mögliche Betätigungsfelder im Bau- und Kunstgewerbe, sollten die amerikanische Industrie, Händler und Produzenten auf die erkannten Defizite im modernen Produktdesign reagieren. Für die Schaufenstergestaltungen des Kaufhauses Saks Fifth Avenue entwirft er in Anlehnung an das *Trägersystem* (Abb. 10) für die Ausstellung von 1924 ein Präsentationsmöbel. Auch hier steht Veränderlichkeit und Multifunktionalität im Vordergrund seines gestalterischen Interesses. (Abb. 11, 12) Es sollten indes fünf Jahre vergehen, ehe Kiesler ein gesamtes Möbelensemble in der ersten Ausstellung der Designervereinigung *AUDAC* einem breiten Publikum vorstellen wird.

Ausstellung und Warenproduktion in Amerika

Als Reaktion auf die „Exposition des Arts Décoratifs et Industriels Modernes" in Paris und die gestiegene Aufmerksamkeit für Produktdesign veranstalten zwischen 1925 und Ende 1929 zahlreiche Warenhäuser in New York Ausstellungen über Kunstgewerbe aus verschiedenen europäischen Ländern. Zunächst gehen die Verantwortlichen nach den Kriterien des Modischen vor, ohne wesentlich zwischen dem Kunsthandwerk des französischen Art Déco und dem avantgardistischen Design des Bauhaus zu unterscheiden.

Das Kaufhaus Wanamaker zeigt bereits 1925 Möbel und Objekte der Pariser Kunstgewerbeschau, während Saks Fifth Avenue beginnt, zeitgenössisches französisches Design anzubieten. Die erste umfassende Präsentation französischer Möbel und Objekte nach dem Pariser Vorbild findet 1927 mit der Ausstellung „Art in Trade" als Kooperation mit dem Metropolitan Museum of Art[11] im Kaufhaus R. H. Macy's in New York statt. 1928 organisiert das Kaufhaus Lord & Taylor mit über 400 Objekten französischer Designer die „Exposition of Modern French Decorative Art", die zu einem durchschlagenden Erfolg wird. Das Haus kann die große Nachfrage trotz des hohen Preisniveaus nur schwer abdecken.[12] Die „International Exposition of Art and Industry" bei R. H. Macy's im gleichen Jahr zählt allein 100.000 Besucher in der ersten Woche und zeigt deutsche, österreichische, italienische, schwedische, französische und amerikanische Designproduktionen. Robert F. Bach, der Direktor des Metropolitan Museums of Art schreibt optimistisch über die Ausstellung: „Diese Ausstellung schließt ein Kapitel in der Geschichte der zeitgenössischen Kunst. Der ‚Modern Style' hat sich etabliert."[13] „Modern Style" bezeichnet eine Mischung aus progressivem europäischen Möbeldesign, sowie der Eleganz großzügiger Formen des Art Déco und begründet damit eine eigene amerikanische Designströmung. Der Architekturkritiker Lewis Mumford beschreibt 1929 den

18

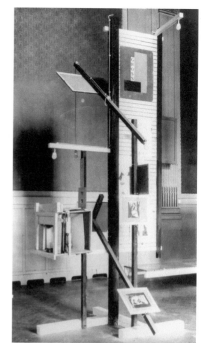

10

11

12

11   Richard G. Wilson, u. a., „The Machine Age and Beyond", in: *The Machine Age in America*, New York 1986, S. 234 ff.
12   Karen Davies, *At Home in Manhattan. Modern Decorative Arts 1925 to the Depression*, New York 1983, S. 86.
13   Ebd. S. 87.

10   *Trägersystem* für die „Internationale Ausstellung

      neuer Theatertechnik", Wien 1924.

      T-System for the "Internationale Ausstellung neu-

      er Theatertechnik", Vienna 1924.

11   Friedrich Kiesler mit flexiblem

      Präsentationsmöbel für Saks Fifth Avenue,

      New York 1927-28.

      Frederick Kiesler with a flexible display stand for

      wares for Saks Fifth Avenue, New York 1927-28.

12   Präsentationsmöbel für Saks Fifth Avenue,

      New York 1927-28.

      Display stand for Saks Fifth Avenue,

      New York 1927-28.

finding a ready market. Maybe Kiesler hoped that moving to New York would allow him to tap into other fields of work in construction and craft, if the American industry, dealers and producers reacted to the identified deficits in modern product design. Based on the *T-System* (Fig. 10) for the 1924 exhibition, he designed a piece of presentation furniture for the Saks Fifth Avenue department store's window display. Once again, changeability and multifunctionality are the focus of his artistic interest. (Fig. 11, 12) However, five years would pass before Kiesler presented a complete set of furniture in the first exhibition of the designers' association *AUDAC* to a wide public.

Exhibition and Production of Commodities in America

As a reaction to the "Exposition des Arts Décoratifs et Industriels Modernes" in Paris and the growing attention to product design, numerous department stores in New York held exhibitions on crafts from various European countries between 1925 and the end of 1929. To begin with, the organizers based the shows on the criteria of fashion, without making any fundamental distinction between the craft work of French Art Déco and the avant-garde design of the Bauhaus.

The Wanamaker department store presented furniture and objects from the Paris art show as early as 1925, while Saks Fifth Avenue started to sell contemporary French design. The first comprehensive presentation of French furniture and objects after the Paris style was the "Art in Trade" exhibition in 1927, a co-operation with the Metropolitan Museum of Art[11] at R. H. Macy's department store in New York. In 1928, the Lord & Taylor store organized the "Exposition of Modern French Decorative Art", featuring more than four hundred objects of French design, which was a sweeping success. In spite of the high prices, the store was hard put to cater for the great demand.[12] The "International Exposition of Art and Industry" at R. H. Macy's the same year drew 100,000 visitors in the first week alone and featured German, Austrian, Italian, Swedish, French, and American design productions. Regarding the exhibition, Robert F. Bach, director of the Metropolitan Museum of Art, wrote optimistically, "This exhibition closes a chapter in the history of contemporary Art. The modern style [...] has come to stay."[13] "Modern Style" refers to a mixture of progressive European furniture design and the elegance of generous forms of Art Déco, and thus designates a distinct American design movement. Architecture critic Lewis Mumford described the effect of Modernism on the American production of goods as follows in 1929: "In January 1927, when I visited Grand Rapids the chief center of furniture production and sales in America, there was but a single suite of modern furniture on the current market: it was an obvious adaption of French work. In the course of two years the whole scene has changed, at least on the surface. [...] The initiative in this change has come chiefly from the big metropolitan department stores [...]. They have held expositions of modern and

11   Richard G. Wilson, et al., "The Machine Age and Beyond", in: *The Machine Age in America,* New York 1986, p. 234 ff.

12   Karen Davies, *At Home in Manhattan. Modern Decorative Arts 1925 to the Depression*, New York 1983, p. 86.

13   Op. cit. p. 87.

Effekt der Moderne auf die amerikanische Warenproduktion, wie folgt: „Als ich im Jänner 1927 Grand Rapids, das führende Zentrum der Möbelherstellung und des Möbelvertriebs in Amerika, besuchte, gab es auf dem aktuellen Markt nur eine einzige Garnitur moderner Möbel: Es handelte sich um eine offensichtliche Adaptierung französischer Arbeit. Im Laufe von zwei Jahren hat sich die ganze Szene verändert, zumindest an der Oberfläche. [...] Die Initiative für diese Veränderung ging in erster Linie von den großen Kaufhäusern in den großen Städten aus [...]. Sie haben Ausstellungen moderner und amerikanischer Arbeiten in einem mehr der weniger großen Rahmen veranstaltet und die Hersteller und kleineren Händler waren nolens volens dazu gezwungen, sich ihnen anzuschließen."[14]

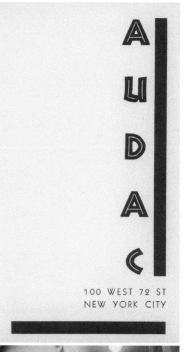

13

American Union of Decorative Arts and Craftsmen *(AUDAC)*

Mit der Gründung der Designervereinigung *AUDAC* reagieren einige New Yorker Architekten und Designer auf die kritiklose Übernahme der in Paris gezeigten überladenen Möbel. Zwei Jahre nach seiner Emigration wird Kiesler 1928 Gründungsmitglied dieser Interessensgemeinschaft.[15] (Abb. 13) Die *AUDAC* steht für die innovativen Impulse der Moderne in der angewandten und bildenden Kunst jener Zeit und setzt sich zum Ziel, „Designer, Architekten und Künstler, die für individuelle Arbeiten, kommerzielle Organisationen, Industriefirmen, Warenhäuser oder Produktionsbüros beauftragt werden, zu vertreten und die Rechte der Designer und deren Nutzungsrechte zu verwalten und so gegen Plagiate zu schützen."[16] Versucht wird die Verbindung der Produktentwicklung und -gestaltung progressiver europäischer Modelle mit dem industriellen Know-how amerikanischer Firmen und die Schaffung eines neuen Selbstverständnisses in den Bereichen Architektur, Möbel- und Produktdesign und der industriellen Warenproduktion.[17]

14

Neben Kiesler gehören die Österreicher Paul Theodore Frankl,[18] sowie Wolfgang und Pola Hoffmann[19] zu der 1931 bereits über hundert Mitglieder zählenden Vereinigung. Die erste Präsentation findet im März 1930 im Grand Central Palace mit dem Titel „Home Show"[20] in Manhattan statt, in jenem Haus, in dem sich auch die Contemporary School of Arts and Crafts befindet und Kiesler zwischen 1929 und 1931 Kurse für Bühnenbild und Schaufensterdesign abhält.[21] (Abb. 14)

Mit Donald Deskey, Willis S. Harrison, Wolfgang und Pola Hoffmann, Friedrich Kiesler und Alexander Kachinsky präsentieren erstmals fünf Mitglieder der Gruppe in der von Kiesler gestalteten Ausstellung jeweils ein komplettes Einrichtungsensemble als Ergebnis ihrer Arbeit. Von den ausgestellten Designern gehört Donald Deskey mit einer Vielzahl an Aufträgen amerikanischer Möbelfabrikanten zu einem

14   Robert A. M. Stern, *New York 1930*, New York 1994, S. 338.
15   Wilson, Pilgrim, Tashjian New York 1986 (wie Anm. 11), S. 296-299.
16   *AUDAC*-Broschüre, 1930/31, Archiv der Kiesler Stiftung Wien.
17   Ebd.
18   Paul T. Frankl wandert bereits 1914 nach Amerika aus, siehe dazu: *Visionäre und Vertriebene*, Mathias Boeckl (Hrsg.), Berlin 1995, S. 88 f.
19   Wolfgang, der Sohn des Architekten Josef Hoffmann, emigriert zeitgleich mit Kiesler nach Amerika. Zum Verhältnis der Künstler, siehe: Boeckl, Berlin 1995 (wie Anm. 18), S. 93-96.
20   John J. Steward, *American Modern*: 1925-1940. *Design for a New Age*, New York 2000, S. 109 ff.
21   Brief von Beatrice Doane Craig an Friedrich Kiesler am 19. Mai 1930, Archiv der Kiesler Stiftung Wien.

13 Broschüre der *AUDAC*, New York 1930-31.

    Brochure of the *AUDAC*, New York 1930-31.

14 Blick in die Ausstellung „Home Show" der

    AUDAC, Grand Central Palace, New York 1930.

    View of the *AUDAC*'s exhibition "Home Show",

    Grand Central Palace, New York 1930.

American work on a more or less grand scale, and, willy-nilly, the manufacturers and the smaller merchants have been forced to join the procession." [14]

American Union of Decorative Arts and Craftsmen *(AUDAC)*

The foundation of the designer association *AUDAC* was the reaction of several New York architects and designers to the uncritical taking over of the florid furniture displayed in Paris. Two years after emigrating, Kiesler became a founding member of this interest group in 1928.[15] (Fig. 13) *AUDAC* stood for the innovative impetus of modernism in the applied and visual arts of the time and aimed to "represent designers, architects and artists commissioned for individual works, commercial organizations, industrial companies, department stores or production offices, and to administer the rights of the designers and their rights of use and thus protect them against plagiarism."[16] The association attempted to combine the product development and design of progressive European models with the industrial expertise of American firms and to create a new identity in the fields of architecture, furniture and product design and industrial production of goods.[17]

In addition to Kiesler, the association, with already more than one hundred members in 1931, included the Austrians Paul Theodore Frankl[18] and Wolfgang and Pola Hoffmann.[19] The first presentation, titled "Home Show",[20] was held at the Grand Central Palace in Manhattan in March 1930 – the same facility that housed the Contemporary School of Arts and Crafts and where Kiesler held courses in stage design and window display design between 1929 and 1931.[21] (Fig. 14)

For the first time, five members of the group, Donald Deskey, Willis S. Harrison, Wolfgang and Pola Hoffmann, Frederick Kiesler, and Alexander Kachinsky, each presented a complete interior as the result of their work at the exhibition designed by Kiesler. Of the designers on show, Donald Deskey was one of the most successful in the nineteen-thirties, with a host of contracts from American furniture manufacturers.[22] The pictures of the exhibition design published in the "Annual of American Design 1931" show design elements that are very horizontal, geared strictly to the layout of the rooms. The letters *AUDAC* were displayed above and in front of every exhibition stand like a logo. Only Kiesler's section was open to visitors and featured studies and photos of projects by American designers on the walls.[23] (Fig. 17, 18, 19) A continuous railing bar

14 Robert A. M. Stern, *New York 1930,* New York 1994, p. 338.

15 Wilson, Pilgrim, Tashjian New York 1986 (cf. note 11), pp. 296-299.

16 *AUDAC* brochure, 1930/31, Archive of the Kiesler Foundation Vienna.

17 Op. cit.

18 Paul T. Frankl emigrated to America as early as 1914, cf.: *Visionäre und Vertriebene,*
    Mathias Boeckl (Ed.), Berlin 1995, p. 88 f.

19 Wolfgang the son of the architect Josef Hoffmann emigrates to America at the same time as Kiesler. On the artists'
    relationship cf.: Boeckl, Berlin 1995 (cf. note 18), p. 93-96.

20 John J. Steward, *American Modern:* 1925-1940. *Design for a New Age,* New York 2000, p. 109 ff.

21 Letter from Beatrice Doane Craig to Frederick Kiesler on May 19, 1930, Archive of the Kiesler Foundation Vienna.

22 Robert A. M. Stern 1994, (cf. note 14), p. 352 ff.

23 For example the window display designs of Thompson and Churchill, etc., cf. Robert L. Leonard, *Annual of American
    Design* 1931, New York 1931, p. 21.

15

15 Blick in die Ausstellung „Home Show" der
   AUDAC, Grand Central Palace, New York 1930
   mit Möbeln von Donald Deskey, Willis S. Harrison
   und Friedrich Kiesler.
   View of the *AUDAC*'s exhibition "Home Show",
   Grand Central Palace, New York 1930 with
   furniture by Donald Deskey, Willis S. Harrison
   and Frederick Kiesler.

16 Blick in die Ausstellung mit Möbeln von Wolfgang
   und Pola Hoffmann und Alexander Kachinsky.
   View of the exhibition with furniture by Wolfgang
   and Pola Hoffmann and Alexander Kachinsky.

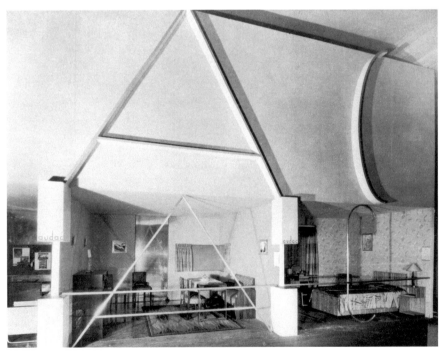

16

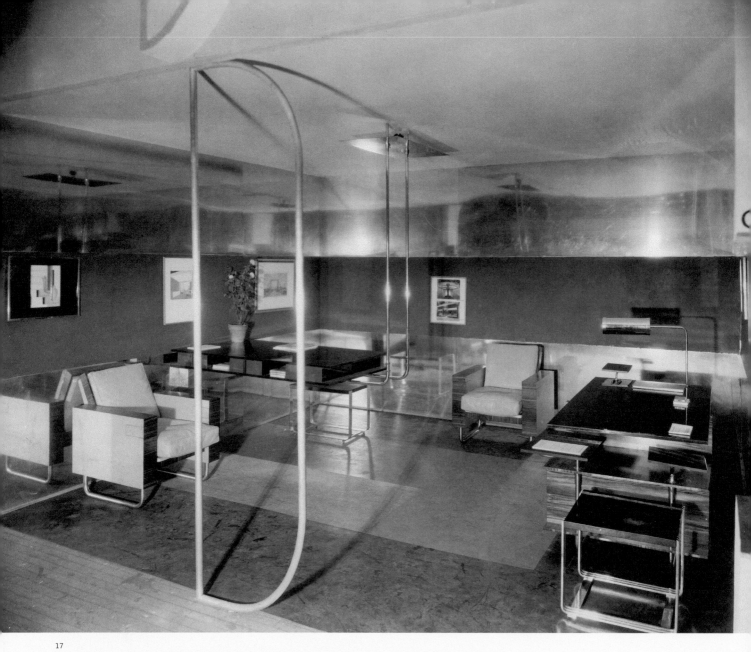

17

17   Kieslers Büroeinrichtung, Blick in die
      Ausstellung der *AUDAC*, New York 1930.
      Foto: Ruth Bernhard.
      Office furniture by Kiesler in the exhibition
      of *AUDAC*, New York 1930.
      Photograph by Ruth Bernhard.

18   Blick in die Ausstellung, Sessel und
      Schreibtisch *Flying Desk*, New York 1930.
      Foto: Ruth Bernhard.
      View of the exhibition, armchair and table
      Flying Desk, New York 1930.
      Photograph by Ruth Bernhard.

18

der erfolgreichsten Designer der 30er Jahre.[22] Die im „Annual of American Design 1931" publizierten Aufnahmen der Ausstellungsgestaltung zeigen stark horizontal ausgerichtete Gestaltungselemente, streng auf die Anordnung der Räume abgestimmt. Die Lettern *AUDAC* werden wie ein Signet oberhalb und vor jede Ausstellungskoje gesetzt. Nur Kieslers Bereich war für Besucher zugänglich und zeigt an den Wänden Studien und Fotos von Projekten amerikanischer Designer.[23] (Abb. 17, 18, 19) Die anderen Räume sind durch eine durchlaufende Geländerstange optisch miteinander verbunden, trennen jedoch den Besucher von den Präsentationsräumen. Die ausgestellten Möbel demonstrieren das neue Anforderungsprofil der *AUDAC*, sie stehen für: „eine Anhebung der Standards im zeitgenössischen Design und für die Entwicklung eines STILS anstelle von verschiedenen Stilen."[24] „Style" ist dabei als Haltung zu verstehen, die auf die Etablierung einer fortschrittlichen, bedürfnisorientierten und industriell gefertigten Möbelproduktion gerichtet ist und sich gegen stilistische Kategorisierungen („styles") wendet. Demnach unterscheiden sich auch die einzelnen Entwürfe der Designer stark voneinander. (Abb. 15, 16)

Kieslers Arbeit fällt durch ihre ganzheitliche Raumgestaltung auf. Die Koje mit ihrer geometrischen, horizontal ausgerichteten Wandgestaltung bildet mit den Einzelmöbeln formal und räumlich eine Einheit und zeigt sich gestalterisch den Ausstellungskonzepten von Wien und Paris verpflichtet. Die Wände sind verchromt und der Schreibtisch *Flying Desk* ist als frei schwebendes Möbel von der Decke abgehängt, das Motiv der *Raumstadt* von Paris 1925 zitierend. (Abb. 17, 18) Zwei *Secretary Chairs* in weißem Leder und Markassa ausgeführt, stehen auf Kufen aus Stahlrohr. Diese abgerundeten Elemente bilden einen Kontrast zu dem geometrisierten Holzkorpus. Die Rückenlehne des Armlehnsessels besteht aus einem beweglichen Holzrahmen, in welchen das Lederkissen eingespannt ist. Ähnlich einem Gleitkanadier scheint die Sitzfläche je nach Stellung der Lehne zu variieren. In den Seiten sind ausklappbare Schubladen eingearbeitet. Ein weiterer Schreibtisch mit drehbaren Elementen und zwei Beistelltische vervollständigen das Ensemble. Im Gegensatz zu den anderen Kojen der Ausstellung geht Kieslers Gestaltung eine enge Verbindung mit dem Raum ein. Veränderlichkeit, Kombinierbarkeit und Bewegung sind die Komponenten, die Kieslers Auffassung einer „Architektur der kontinuierlichen Spannung (Tensionism)"[25] im Objekthaften manifestieren.

Vom Umgang mit moderner Kunst

Friedrich Kiesler publiziert 1930 sein Buch *Contemporary Art Applied to the Store and Its Display* (Abb. 20), das bereits 1929 fertig gestellt wird. Er schreibe dieses Buch, „weil das Land überhäuft wurde mit armseligen und falschen Beispielen des Modernismus [...] [und weil] der plötzliche Einfluss von zeitgenössischer Kunst es notwendig macht, die wirklichen Werte und Bedeutungen [von kreativem Gestalten, Anm. d. A.] zu kontrollieren."[26] Kiesler bezieht sich dabei auch auf die

22 Robert A. M. Stern 1994, (wie Anm. 14), S. 352 ff.
23 Wie etwa die Schaufenstergestaltungen von Thompson and Churchill u. a., siehe Robert L. Leonard, *Annual of American Design* 1931, New York 1931, S. 21.
24 Siehe Broschüre *AUDAC* 1930/31, Archiv der Kiesler Stiftung Wien.
25 Dieser Begriff taucht erstmals in Kieslers „Manifest, Vitalbau – Raumstadt – Funktionelle Architektur" auf, publiziert in: *NB De Stijl*, 6, 1925, S. 141 ff.
26 Frederick Kiesler, *Contemporary Art Applied to The Store and Its Display*, New York 1930, S. 18.

visually linked the other rooms with each other but separated visitors from the presentation rooms. The furniture exhibits demonstrated the new requirement profile of the *AUDAC*, they stood for: "elevation of standards in contemporary design and for the development of a STYLE rather than styles."[24] Where "style" should be understood as the effort to establish a progressive, need-oriented and industrial furniture production, opposing stylistic categorizations. Accordingly, the individual designs are extremely different. (Fig. 15, 16)

Kiesler's work stands out due to its holistic design of the interior. The stand with its geometrical, horizontal wall design forms a formal and spatial whole with the individual pieces of furniture, and bespeaks its indebtedness to the exhibition concepts of Vienna and Paris in terms of design. The walls are chromium-plated and the *Flying Desk* is a hovering piece of furniture suspended from the ceiling, citing the theme of the *City in Space* of Paris 1925. (Fig. 17, 18) Two *Secretary Chairs* in white leather and Macassar are based on steel-tube runners. These rounded elements contrast with the geometrical wooden body. The backrest of the armrest chair consists of a movable wooden frame with the leather cushion stretched across it. Much like a gliding canoe, the seat seems to vary depending on the position of the backrest. Fold-out drawers are built into the sides. Another desk with swiveling elements and two side-tables round off the set. Unlike the other stands at the exhibition, Kiesler's design links up intimately with the setting. Variability, combinability and movement are the design components that manifest Kiesler's conception of an "architecture of continuous tensionism"[25] in the object.

Handling of Modern Art

In 1930, Frederick Kiesler published his book *Contemporary Art Applied to the Store and Its Display* (Fig. 20), that he had already completed in 1929. He wrote this book, he said, "because the country was being inundated with pathetic, false examples of modernism [...] [and because] the sudden influence of contemporary art make it necessary to review the real values and meanings [of creative design, author's note]."[26] Here, Kiesler is also referring to the numerous presentations of contemporary arts and crafts with examples of French Art Déco, its adaptations and American variations, in New York and Chicago, primarily opposing the indiscriminate appropriation of modern design, without regard for established principles of modern design. The book features numerous examples of European avant-garde art movements in the fields of window display design, exhibition design, object and furniture design, and architecture designs. According to Kiesler, visual art and applied art are aesthetic expressions of various contents of consciousness of which the visitor to the museum and the company manager alike must take advantage. In his opinion, the possibility of mass production by machines allows the creation of a new

24   Cf. *AUDAC* brochure 1930/31, Archive of the Kiesler Foundation Vienna.
25   This term first appeared in Kiesler's "Manifest, Vitalbau – Raumstadt – Funktionelle Architektur", published in: *NB De Stijl*, 6, 1925, p. 141 ff.
26   Frederick Kiesler, *Contemporary Art Applied to The Store and Its Display*, New York 1930, p. 18.

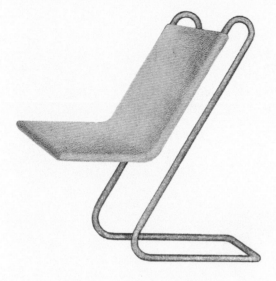

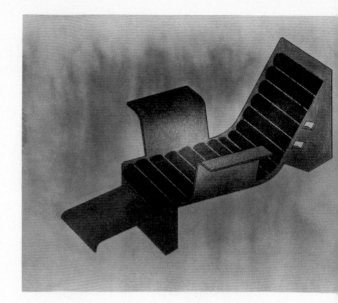

A metal tubing chair. The elasticity of the
construction eliminates the need of cushions.
This design no longer resembles the wooden
chair.
F. KIESLER, architect (New York)

Sheet-Furniture. Deck chair, cut from one
piece of sheet material. First reproduction.
F. KIESLER, architect (New York)

19

19 Entwürfe für einen Stahlrohrsessel und einen
Liegestuhl, publiziert in: *Contemporary Art
Applied to the Store and Its Display,* New York 1930.
Sketches for tubular steel chair and a deckchair,
published in: *Contemporary Art Applied to the
Store and Its Display,* New York 1930.

20 Umschlag, *Contemporary Art Applied to the
Store and Its Display,* New York 1930.
Cover, *Contemporary Art Applied to the Store
and Its Display,* New York 1930.

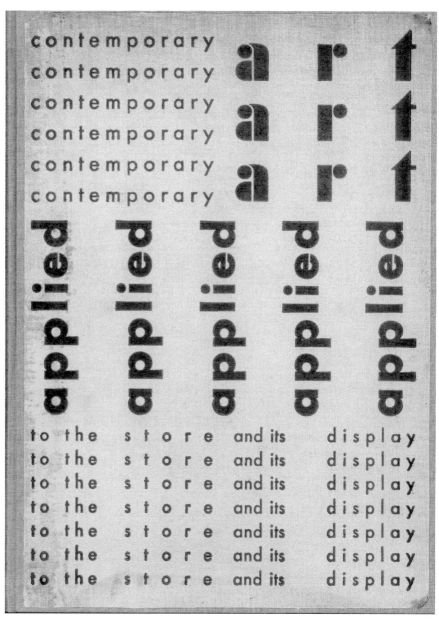

20

zahlreichen in New York und Chicago stattfindenden Präsentationen zeitgenössischen Kunstgewerbes mit Beispielen des französischen Art Déco, seinen Abwandlungen und amerikanischen Spielarten und wendet sich in erster Linie gegen die undifferenzierte Aneignung modernen Designs, ohne Rücksicht auf die bereits bekannten Gestaltungsprinzipien der Moderne. Das Buch umfasst zahlreiche Beispiele europäischer Kunstströmungen der Avantgarde aus den Bereichen Schaufensterdesign, Ausstellungsgestaltung, Objekt- und Möbeldesign, sowie Architekturentwürfe. Bildende Kunst und angewandte Kunst sind nach Kiesler ästhetische Äußerungen verschiedener Bewusstseinsinhalte, die sich der Museumsbesucher genauso wie der Geschäftsmanager zu Nutze machen soll. Die Möglichkeit der Massenproduktion durch die Maschine ermöglicht seiner Meinung nach die Schaffung einer neuen, dem Menschen dienenden amerikanischen Kunst. „Wenn je ein Land die Chance hatte, eine Kunst für sein Volk, durch sein Volk zu schaffen, nicht durch Einzelpersonen und das Kunsthandwerk, sondern durch maschinelle Massenproduktion, dann ist es das Amerika von heute. Dies wird durch Adaptierung und Wiedergeburt geschehen und zutiefst amerikanisch sein."[27]

Ein Teil seines Buches *Contemporary Art Applied to the Store and Its Display* widmet sich explizit dem Möbeldesign. Neben zwei eigenen Entwürfen für Sitzmöbel (Abb. 19) publiziert Kiesler drei Stahlrohrmöbel, Sinnbild moderner Materialaneignung, zur Verdeutlichung alternativer Konstruktionsmethoden: Zwei Freischwinger von Mies van der Rohe, sowie das Modell B5 von Marcel Breuer von 1928. (Abb. 21) Wie die Modelle Mies Van der Rohes ist auch Kieslers Stahlrohrmodell durch eine einzige durchlaufende Stahlrohrverbindung und eine frei schwingende Sitzfläche gekennzeichnet. Die abgebildeten Modelle Kieslers stellen eher Studien als fertig ausgereiftes und erprobtes Design dar. Die Gefahr des Nach-vorne-kippens scheint augenfällig. Kiesler betont, dass durch die neuen Materialien auch jede Ähnlichkeit zu traditionellen Konstruktionsmethoden hinfällig werde. Im zweiten Entwurf, dem Liegestuhl, beschreibt Kiesler die Form als Folge von gebogenen, durchgängig laminierten Holzschichten. Die Möglichkeiten von laminiertem Sperrholz machen sich um 1930 Marcel Breuer, sowie später Charles und Ray Eames in ihren Modellen zur Ausstellung „Organic Architecture" im MoMA 1940 zu Nutze.

Contemporary Art Applied to the Store and Its Display entsteht zeitgleich mit Paul T. Frankls Buch *Form and Re-Form*.[28] Frankl, schon 1914 nach seinem Studium an der Wiener Technischen Hochschule nach New York emigriert und daher nicht der europäischen Denkschule der 20er Jahre verhaftet, ist ebenfalls Mitglied der *AUDAC* und mit Friedrich Kiesler freundschaftlich verbunden. (Abb. 22) Frankls Möbelentwürfe sind noch stärker dem secessionistischen Stil der Wiener Werkstätte um die Jahrhundertwende verpflichtet. In seiner Publikation reiht der Designer Frankl wichtige Themen zeitgenössischer Gestaltung didaktisch aneinander. Kiesler hingegen sucht in seiner Abhandlung nach einer Erklärung für die inneren Zusammenhänge der verschiedenen Artikulationen moderner Gestaltung, der bildenden Kunst, der Architektur, dem Ausstellungs- und Produktdesign. Seine

27   Ebd. S. 67 ff.
28   Siehe dazu, Boeckl Berlin 1995 (wie Anm. 18).

21 Stahlrohrstühle von Marcel Breuer und Mies van
    der Rohe, publiziert in: *Contemporary Art Applied
    to the Store and Its Display*, New York 1930.
    Tubular steel chairs by Marcel Breuer and
    Mies van der Rohe, published in: *Contemporary
    Art Applied to the Store and Its Display*,
    New York 1930.

22 Portrait von Paul Theodore Frankl, gewidmet
    Friedrich Kiesler, New York um 1930.
    Photo portrait of Paul Theodore Frankl,
    inscribed to Frederick Kiesler, New York c. 1930.

American art in the service of mankind. "If ever a country has had the chance to create an art for its people, through its people, not through individuals and handicrafts, but through machine mass production, that country is America today. It will be adaption and a rebirth. It will be American."[27]

Part of his book *Contemporary Art Applied to the Store and Its Display* is dedicated explicitly to furniture design. In addition to two of his own seat furniture designs, (Fig. 19) Kiesler published three pieces of steel-tube furniture, a symbol of the appropriation of modern material, in order to illustrate alternative methods of construction: two cantilever chairs by Mies van der Rohe and the B5 model by Marcel Breuer of 1928. (Fig. 21) Like Mies van der Rohe's models, Kiesler's steel-tube model was also characterized by a single continuous steel-tube connection and a cantilevered seat. Kiesler's models depicted in the book are studies rather than fully developed, tested design. The danger of tipping over forward seems obvious. Kiesler emphasized that the new materials invalidated any similarity to traditional methods of construction. In the second design, the deckchair, Kiesler described the form as a sequence of curved, continuously laminated layers of wood. Around 1930, Marcel Breuer, and later Charles and Ray Eames took advantage of the possibilities offered by laminated plywood in their models for the exhibition "Organic Architecture" at the MoMA in 1940.

Contemporary Art Applied to the Store and Its Display was written at the same time as Paul T. Frankl's book *Form and Re-Form*.[28] Frankl, having already emigrated to New York in 1914 after graduating from Vienna's University of Technology, and thus not being a captive of the European school of thought of the nineteen-twenties, was also a member of *AUDAC* and on friendly terms with Frederick Kiesler. (Fig. 22) Frankl's furniture designs were even more strongly indebted to the Secessionist style of the Wiener Werkstätten around the turn of the century. In his publication, the designer Frankl didactically lined up important topics of contemporary design. In his treatise, Frederick Kiesler, on the other hand, set out to find an explanation for the inner relationships of the different articulations of modern design, visual art, architecture, exhibition and product design. His publication constituted an important contribution to the American discussion on the reception of European modernism and attempted to offer the reader a strategy for appropriating the complex associations between the various disciplines. At the same time, Kiesler referred to his own activity as a European avant-garde artist, revealing himself to be an expert on the American architecture and design scene. In autumn 1929, shortly after completing his book, Kiesler's hopes to obtain lucrative contracts were dashed by the New York stock-market crash. In summer of the following year, he traveled to Paris where he met numerous friends and colleagues, protagonists of European modernism: Theo van Doesburg, Piet Mondrian, Hans Arp, Hans Richter, Mies van der Rohe and Fernand Léger, as well as Le Corbusier. The 8th international arts and crafts show, the "Exposition des Arts Décoratifs", was taking place in

27 Op. cit. p. 67 ff.
28 Cf. Boeckl Berlin 1995 (cf. note 18).

Schrift stellt einen wichtigen Beitrag zur amerikanischen Diskussion über die Rezeption der europäischen Moderne dar und versucht dem Leser, eine Strategie zur Aneignung der komplexen Zusammenhänge der diversen Disziplinen anzubieten. Gleichzeitig verweist Kiesler auf seine eigene Tätigkeit als europäischer Avantgarde-Künstler und exponiert sich als Kenner der amerikanischen Architektur- und Designszene. Im Herbst 1929, kurz nach Fertigstellung des Buches, wird Kieslers Hoffnung auf lukrative Aufträge durch den New Yorker Börsenkrach zerstört. Im Sommer des folgenden Jahres reist er nach Paris und trifft dort zahlreiche Freunde und Kollegen, Protagonisten der europäischen Moderne: Theo van Doesburg, Piet Mondrian, Hans Arp, Hans Richter, Mies van der Rohe und Fernand Léger, ebenso wie Le Corbusier. Zu jener Zeit findet die 8. Internationale Kunstgewerbeschau „Exposition des Arts Décoratifs" in Paris statt. Walter Gropius leitet die deutsche Sektion und präsentiert die neuesten Entwicklungen im Bereich des Möbeldesigns und des Wohnungsbaus.[29] Ob die Treffen Kieslers mit Mies van der Rohe im Zusammenhang mit den Konzeptionen neuester Produktentwicklung stehen, ist uns nicht überliefert. Aus New York erreicht Kiesler vom Architekten Wallace K. Harrison die Nachricht, zum Lektor an der School of Architecture der Columbia University ernannt worden zu sein.[30] Kiesler kehrt nach New York zurück, wo er seine Position gestärkt sieht und nun hofft, seine Tätigkeitsfelder erweitern zu können.

ES IST TAG GEWORDEN …

Die 1933 stattfindende „Chicago World's Fair", auch „Century of Progress Exhibition" genannt, steht sinnbildlich für Amerikas erneuten wirtschaftlichen Aufschwung. Am 8. Januar dieses Jahres reist Kiesler mit seinem Freund und späteren Galeristen Sidney Janis (Janowitz) nach Grand Rapids in Michigan und Chicago. Er schreibt an seine Frau Steffi bereits am 10. Januar aus Chicago: „Haben konstant Konferenzen mit einem bestimmten Manufacturer. Situation ist gut."[31] Dabei erwähnt er auch einen Termin zum Lunch mit dem Direktor des Art Institute in Chicago am 11. Januar. In Briefen berichtet Kiesler vom Besuch der „Chicago World's Fair" und von Treffen mit Museumsleuten, sowie einem ersten Kontakt mit der Firma Sears & Roebuck, um über die Realisierung eines Einfamilienhauses, dem *Nucleus House*, zu verhandeln.[32] Im selben Schreiben stellt er jedoch fest, dass diese Reise vor allem seiner Möbelproduktion gewidmet sein soll. Am 17. Januar reist Kiesler erneut nach Grand Rapids in Michigan, um dort weitere Vertreter von Möbelfabrikanten zu treffen. „Haben heute wichtige Manufacturers gesehen. Wir sind hier überall gut eingeführt und empfangen [worden]. Morgen sehe [ich] andere Manufacturer – hoffe auch einen wegen Housing."[33] (Abb. 24) Kiesler hält in dieser Zeit zahllose Vorträge auf Meetings. „Ich denke in den Pausen automatisch an unsere Lage, wie irrsinnig, dass so viel wie nichts in 6 Jahren in New York geschah!"[34] Einen ersten Erfolg übermittelt Kiesler seiner

29 Walter Gropius, *Section Allemande*, Deutscher Beitrag zur „Exposition des Arts decoratifs", Paris 1930.
30 *Friedrich Kiesler 1890-1965*, Dieter Bogner (Hrsg.), Wien 1988, S. 53.
31 Brief von Kiesler an Steffi Kiesler am 10. Januar 1933, Archiv der Kiesler Stiftung Wien.
32 Brief von Friedrich Kiesler an Steffi Kiesler vom 15. Januar 1933, Archiv der Kiesler Stiftung Wien.
33 Brief von Friedrich Kiesler an Steffi Kiesler vom 17. Januar 1933, Archiv der Kiesler Stiftung Wien.
34 Brief von Friedrich Kiesler an Steffi Kiesler vom 21. Januar 1933, Archiv der Kiesler Stiftung Wien.

23 Brief Kieslers an seine Frau Steffi mit einer
    Karikatur zu seinen Vorträgen in Chicago,
    Januar 1933.
    Letter from Kiesler to his wife Steffi with a
    caricatural drawing of his lectures in Chicago,
    January 1933.

Paris at the time. Walter Gropius headed the German section, presenting the latest developments in furniture design and housing construction.[29] We do not know whether Kiesler's meetings with Mies van der Rohe were connected with the conceptions for the latest product development. From New York, Kiesler received news from the architect Wallace K. Harrison that he had been appointed junior university teacher at Columbia University's School of Architecture.[30] Kiesler returned to New York, seeing his position strengthened and hoping to extend his fields of work.

IT HAS DAWNED …

The "Chicago World's Fair," also referred to as the "Century of Progress Exhibition," held in 1933, was symbolic of America's renewed economic upturn. On January 8 of that year, Kiesler traveled to Grand Rapids in Michigan and Chicago with his friend and later gallerist Sidney Janis (Janowitz). Already on January 10, he wrote to Steffi from Chicago, "We are having constant meetings with a certain manufacturer. The situation is good."[31] He also mentioned a lunch appointment with the director of the Art Institute in Chicago on January 11. In letters, Kiesler reported on his visit to the "Chicago World's Fair" and on meetings with museum people, and his first contact with a company called Sears & Roebuck with the aim of negotiating the design of a family house, the *Nucleus House*.[32] In the same letter, however, he observed that this journey was above all to be dedicated to his furniture production. Accordingly, Kiesler traveled to Grand Rapids in Michigan on January 17 again in order to meet further representatives of furniture manufacturers. "Met important manufacturers today. We were well accepted and received everywhere. Seeing other manufacturers tomorrow – hopefully one about housing, too."[33] (Fig. 24) Kiesler held countless lectures at meetings during this time. "During the breaks, I automatically think about our situation, how crazy that next to nothing has happened in New York in six years!"[34] On August 19 of the same year, Kiesler reports on a first success to his wife, writing, "IT HAS DAWNED … found a telegram from Chicago: my contract accepted, 'Proceed Chicago at once' is the laconic American telegram from the biggest lamp company, saying that they need me."[35] However, the contract as a designer for Rembrandt Lamps was the sole economic success of his efforts.

In January 1934, Kiesler also held lectures at a furniture exhibition in Chicago. "The difference between Good and Bad Modern Design",[36] the title of the show, was intended to achieve greater acceptance of modern product design. The contemporary design symposium initiated by the furniture exhibition, the *Clinic for Modern Design*, was intended primarily as a promotional

33

29 Walter Gropius, *Section Allemande*, German contribution to the "Exposition des Arts decoratifs", Paris 1930.
30 *Friedrich Kiesler 1890-1965*, Dieter Bogner (Ed.), Wien 1988, p. 53.
31 Letter from Frederick Kiesler to Steffi Kiesler on January 10, 1933, Archive of the Kiesler Foundation Vienna. (Orig. quot. in Ger.)
32 Letter from Frederick Kiesler to Steffi Kiesler on January 15, 1933, Archive of the Kiesler Foundation Vienna.
33 Letter from Frederick Kiesler to Steffi Kiesler on January 17, 1933, Archive of the Kiesler Foundation Vienna. (Orig. quot. in Ger.)
34 Letter from Frederick Kiesler to Steffi Kiesler on January 21, 1933, Archive of the Kiesler Foundation Vienna. (Orig. quot. in Ger.)
35 Letter from Frederick Kiesler to Steffi Kiesler on August 19, 1933, Archive of the Kiesler Foundation Vienna. (Orig. quot. in Ger.)
36 "Modern Home Furnishings talks at Mart Tonight", in: *Chicago Journal of Commerce*, January 3, 1934.

Frau am 19. August desselben Jahres als er schreibt: „ES IST TAG GEWORDEN ...
fand Telegramm aus Chicago vor: Mein Kontrakt angenommen ‚Proceed Chicago at
once' das lakonische amerikanische Telegramm der größten Lampenfirma, dass sie
mich brauchen."[35] Der Vertrag als Designer für die Firma Rembrandt Lamps bleibt
jedoch der einzige wirtschaftliche Erfolg seiner Bemühungen.

Im Januar 1934 hält Kiesler auch Vorträge im Rahmen einer Chicagoer Möbelmesse. „The difference between Good and Bad Modern Design",[36] so der Titel, soll
der Schaffung einer besseren Akzeptanz moderner Produktgestaltung dienen. Das
von der Möbelmesse ins Leben gerufene Symposium für zeitgenössisches Design,
die *Clinic for Modern Design* dient in erster Linie als Werbeveranstaltung für Fabri-
kanten und Kunden. Kiesler nützt dieses Forum um seine Thesen einer breiteren
Öffentlichkeit vorzustellen. Der Designer sei damit betraut, die neuen Errungen-
schaften der Technologie gestalterisch umzusetzen oder in Zusammenarbeit mit
Technikern gewisse Neuerungen als Impulse für die Forschung verfügbar zu
machen. Der Designer arbeite als Gestalter an der Schnittstelle von Technologie
und Sozialwissenschaft und seine Arbeit soll in erster Linie auf die Verbesserung
der Lebensverhältnisse ausgerichtet sein.

Erstmals taucht in dieser Zeit der Begriff der *Design-Correlation* auf.[37]
Kiesler erläutert den Zusammenhang von gutem Design im Alltag anhand des
Alltagsobjektes der Badewanne. Im Besonderen geht er auf die Probleme der
praktischen Nutzung ein, die erst in der Handhabe entstehen, wie etwa dem Aus-
rutschen auf einer zu glatten Oberfläche.[38] Kiesler begreift Design als die Wissenschaft vom Zusammenspiel der sozialen, technischen und natürlichen Verhältnisse,
in die der Mensch agierend eingebunden ist. Sein Verständnis von moderner
Produktgestaltung, das sich vor allem nach der Funktionalität des Objektes
richtet, kommt auch in seinen Möbelentwürfen jener Zeit zur Anwendung.

34   Am 17. Oktober 1933 eröffnet die Modernage Furniture Company ihr Haus
mit einem Prototyp von Kieslers *Space House* und Möbeln u. a. von Gilbert Rhode.[39]
(Abb. 25-28) Die Eröffnung steht im Zeichen der Neuorientierung mit Beispielen
Modernen Möbeldesigns im Gegensatz zu den bisher vertretenen Produkten des
Art Déco französischer Prägung. Ausgestattet mit modernen Möbeln ist das *Space
House* als Ausstellungsinstallation gleichsam ein modellhaftes Beispiel für Kieslers
Architekturverständnis. Mit dieser Arbeit versucht Kiesler erstmals, seine Vorstel-
lung einer selbst tragenden Schalenkonstruktion als Umsetzung seiner *Zeit-Raum-
Architektur* [40] zu verwirklichen. Sein Interesse ist auf die Zusammenhänge zwi-
schen der Dynamik des Wohnens, der Möglichkeit der Anpassung an sich verän-
dernde Lebenssituationen, sowie auf die veränderliche Größe der in einem Haus-

35   Brief von Friedrich Kiesler an Steffi Kiesler vom 19. August 1933, Archiv der Kiesler Stiftung Wien.

36   „Modern Home Furnishings talks at Mart Tonight", in: *Chicago Journal of Commerce*, 3. Januar 1934.

37   Bogner 1988 (wie Anm. 31), S. 67.

38   Kiesler untersucht das Verhalten in der Badewanne, das Greifen nach der Seife, Verändern der Temperatur, Hinsetzen zur
     Entspannung, Aufstehen und Verlassen der Wanne. „It is impossible to stand, to sit, to lay down [...] it would not be so difficult
     to put a wider rim along the bathtub, to be able to sit, to lay a washer or accessoires [...] reading brings us to the question of
     proper light [...] Leisure and relaxation are not considered at all." Friedrich Kiesler, „We are on a Threshold Of a New Era of
     Progressive Design", in: *Retailing, Home Furnishings Edition*, 29. Januar 1934.

39   Elizabeth M'Rae Boykin, „Current Displays Afford Many Suggestions for Furnishing Pleasant Homes",
     in: *New York Sun*, 23. Oktober 1933.

40   Kiesler verwendet den Begriff „Time-Space-Architecture" erstmals 1925 und bezieht sich in seinen theoretischen Texten nach
     1933 immer wieder darauf. Siehe dazu Bogner 1988 (wie Anm. 31), S. 230-242.

24   *Space House*, übermalter Andruck,

New York 1939.

Space House, painted print, New York 1939.

show for manufacturers and customers. Kiesler took advantage of this forum in order to present his theories to a wider public. The designer, he maintained, is entrusted with translating the latest technological achievements into design or, in co-operation with engineers, to make certain innovations available as impetus for research. The designer works at the interface of technology and social science and his work should be geared first and foremost to improving living conditions.

The concept of *Design-Correlation* first appeared during this time.[37] Kiesler explained the context of good design in everyday life on the basis of the everyday bathtub object. Specifically he went into the problems of practical use, that arise only when the object is used, for example slipping up on a surface that is too smooth.[38] Kiesler regarded design as the science of the interplay of social, technological and natural conditions in which man is embedded as an actor. His understanding of modern product design, geared above all to the functionality of the object, was also applied in his furniture designs at that time.

The Modernage Furniture Company opened shop on October 17, 1933, with a prototype of Kiesler's *Space House* and furniture by Gilbert Rhode.[39] (Fig. 25-28) The opening focused on reorientation, with examples of modern furniture design in contrast to the French-style Art Déco products previously exhibited. Furnished with modern furniture, the *Space House* is both an exhibition installation and a modeled example of Kiesler's understanding of architecture. (Fig. 24) With this work, Kiesler set out for the first time to realize his idea of a self-supporting shell structure as an implementation of his *Time-Space-Architecture*.[40] He was interested in the links between the dynamics of living, the possibility of adapting to changing situations in life, and the changing size of the community living in a household. Kiesler saw all of these social parameters realized in his *Space House* both in terms of design and architecture. Formally, his theoretical approach was reflected in the rounded sides of the house. A change of form that went back to the *Endless Theater*, at the same time referring to the furniture and architectural designs of the coming years. Kiesler's suggestion of a house with flexible partition walls, similar to those of the *Nucleus House* of 1931, in order to vary the size of the rooms depending on the situation and space required, met with great approval in the press and the public.[41] (Fig. 28)

The *Space House* is not only the presentation of an extraordinary building concept but also the venue for a temporary exhibition of modern European art.

35

37   Bogner 1988 (cf. note 31), p. 67.

38   Kiesler analyzed behavior in the bathtub, reaching for the soap, changing the temperature, sitting down to relax, standing up and getting out of the bathtub. "It is impossible to stand, to sit, to lay down [...] it would not be so difficult to put a wider rim along the bathtub, to be able to sit, to lay a washer or accessoires [...] reading brings us to the question of proper light [...] Leisure and relaxation are not considered at all." Friedrich Kiesler, "We are on a Threshold Of a New Era of Progressive Design", in: *Retailing, Home Furnishings Edition*, 29. Januar 1934.

39   Elizabeth M'Rae Boykin, "Current Displays Afford Many Suggestions for Furnishing Pleasant Homes", in: *New York Sun*, Oktober 23, 1933.

40   Kiesler uses the term "Time-Space-Architecture" for the first time in 1925, and refers to it on many occasions in his theoretical writings after 1933. Cf. Bogner 1988 (cf. note 31), p. 230-242.

41   "Space House Gives a Peep into Future", in: *NY American*, Oktober 17, 1933; "Space House exhibited", in: *New York Times*, Oktober 17, 1933; "Space House Shown", in: *New York Times*, Oktober 17, 1933.

25   *Space House* im Verkaufslokal der

Modernage Furniture Company,

New York 1933. Foto: Fay S. Lincoln.

The *Space House* in the shop of Modernage

Furniture Company, New York 1933.

Photograph by Fay S. Lincoln.

26-27   Blick ins *Space House*, New York 1933.

Foto: Fay S. Lincoln.

View into *Space House*, New York 1933.

Photograph by Fay S. Lincoln.

26

27

28

29

halt lebenden Gemeinschaft gerichtet. All diese sozialen Parameter sieht Kiesler in seinem *Space House* gestalterisch und architektonisch realisiert. Formal schlägt sich sein theoretischer Ansatz in den abgerundeten Seiten des Hauses nieder. Ein Gestaltwandel, der auf das *Endless Theater* zurückgreift und gleichzeitig auf die Möbel und Architekturentwürfe der kommenden Jahre verweist. Kieslers Vorschlag eines Hauses mit flexiblen Zwischenwänden, ähnlich denen im *Nucleus House* von 1931, um die Raumgröße je nach Situation und benötigtem Platz variabel zu gestalten, findet bei der Presse und dem Publikum großen Anklang.[41] (Abb. 28)

Das *Space House* ist nicht nur die Präsentation eines außerordentlichen Gebäudekonzepts, sondern auch Ort einer temporären Ausstellung europäischer Kunst der Moderne. Alfred Auerbach, Kritiker und Freund Friedrich Kieslers, beschreibt die Eröffnung des *Space House* wie folgt: „Für die Eröffnung brachte eine Leihausstellung mit Gemälden von Picasso, Léger, Gorky, Mondrian und anderen kräftige Farbelemente in die Räume. Einen weiteren Höhepunkt bildete eine Skulptur von Brancusi. Dazwischen hoben sich die Möbel und getischlerten Stücke und Lampen der Interieurs deutlich vom neutralen Weiß des Hintergrunds ab und boten so den vielleicht passendsten Rahmen für moderne Einrichtungsgegenstände, der hier je gesehen wurde."[42] In seiner Doppelfunktion als Einfamilienhaus und Ausstellungsarchitektur, erweist sich Kieslers *Space House* als gelungene Verbindung von Raum, Interieur und Kunst. Kiesler erzielt durch die neutralen weißen Wände einen wahrnehmungstechnischen Effekt der Nobilitierung des Alltagsgegenstandes. Diese doppelte Konnotation von Kunstwerk und Alltagsobjekt im neutralen Ausstellungsraum stellt damit einen frühen Beitrag zur Debatte über den Ausstellungsraum als *White Cube* dar. Auerbach beschreibt Kieslers Umsetzung seiner Idee von ineinander greifenden Raumfunktionen im *Space House* als ausgewogene Einheit. Ein Konzept, das Kiesler in der Auseinandersetzung mit der Möblierung und der Raumstruktur in der *Art of This Century* Gallery erneut 1942 unter Beweis stellen wird.

38

Die Einrichtung für Mergentime

Kieslers bereits erwähnte Reise nach Chicago und Grand Rapids 1933 steht auch in Verbindung mit dem Auftrag für Charles und Marguerite Mergentime, eine komplette Wohnzimmereinrichtung zu gestalten.[43] Im August 1933 schreibt er an seine Frau Steffi, dass er an den Entwürfen arbeite, „so dass Mergentime diese Woche noch den [sic!] vollständigen Layout des Apartments haben werden."[44] (Abb. 30) Marguerite Mergentime ist Textildesignerin und zu jener Zeit selbst Mitglied der

41 „Space House Gives a Peep into Future", in: *NY American*, 17. Oktober 1933; „Space House exhibited", in: *New York Times*, 17. Oktober 1933; „Space House Shown", in: *New York Times*, 17. Oktober 1933.

42 Alfred Auerbach „Architecture And Decoration Are Wed In 'The Space House'", in: *Retailing, Home Furnishing Edition*, 23. Oktober 1933, S. 3. In einer weiteren Kritik hebt Auerbach beide Wandbilder, ein abstraktes und ein figuratives hervor, welche in die Architektur und die Ausstellung integriert sind.

43 Im Januar 1933 trifft Kiesler einige Repräsentanten großer Möbelfabrikanten, etwa der Baker Furniture Inc., für die der amerikanische Designer Donald Deskey arbeitet, sowie die Firma Kroehler Furniture. In den erneut verbesserten wirtschaftlichen Bedingungen sieht Kiesler gute Chancen, Aufträge als Produktdesigner zu bekommen.
In der Literatur finden wir verschiedene Vornamen und auch verschiedene Schreibweisen des Nachnamens als Mergentine und Mergentime auf. In der Broschüre der *AUDAC* ist sie als Marguerita Mergentime angeführt.

44 Brief von Friedrich Kiesler an Steffi Kiesler, undatiert, Archiv der Kiesler Stiftung Wien.

Space House, Plan zur Innenansicht,

New York 1933.

Space House, perspective view, New York 1933.

29 Blick ins *Space House*, mit Brancusis *Oiseau*

dans l'espace 1932-1940 (linke),

New York 1933.

View into *Space House* with Brancusi's *Oiseau*

dans l'espace 1932-1940 (left),

New York 1933.

Alfred Auerbach, critic and friend of Frederick Kiesler's, described the opening of the *Space House* as follows, "For the opening a loan exhibition of paintings by Picasso, Léger, Gorky, Mondrian and others sparked up the rooms with vivid pools of color interest. A Brancusi sculpture was another highspot. Amidst these the furniture and carpenting and lamps of the interiors stood out in clear relief against the neutral white of the background to afford the most satisfactory setting for modern home furnishings that has perhaps yet been seen here."[42] In its dual function as a house and exhibition architecture, Kiesler's *Space House* proved to be an accomplished combination of space, interior and art. By means of the neutral white walls, Kiesler achieved a perceptual effect of ennobling the everyday object. This double connotation of art work and everyday object in the neutral exhibition space thus constituted an early contribution to the debate on the exhibition space as a *White Cube*. Auerbach described Kiesler's realization of his idea of intermeshing spatial functions in the *Space House* as a balanced unified whole. A concept that Kiesler was to demonstrate in an exhibition context with his furniture and space structure at the *Art of This Century* Gallery once again in 1942.

Furnishings for Mergentime

Kiesler's aforementioned trip to Chicago and Grand Rapids in 1933 was also connected with the contract for Charles and Marguerite Mergentime to design a complete set of sitting-room furnishings.[43] In August 1933, he wrote to his wife Steffi that he was working on the plans, "so that Mergentime will already get the complete layout for the apartment this week."[44] (Fig. 30) Marguerite Mergentime was a textile designer and herself a member of *AUDAC* at the time.[45] The plans were not actually carried out until summer 1935.[46] (Fig. 31) At the same time, Nelson Rockefeller was having his apartment converted by Wallace K. Harrison, another member of *AUDAC* and friend of Frederick Kiesler's. Kiesler's aim in visiting Mergentime's apartment with the architect Philip Johnson and Rockefeller Jr. was to promote his own furniture design.[47] We can assume that he was counting on getting more contracts at that time. At the start of 1936, he filed patents for various pieces of furniture from the set, including the *Party Lounge*.[48] (Fig. 32)

39

42 Alfred Auerbach "Architecture And Decoration Are Wed In 'The Space House'", in: *Retailing, Home Furnishing Edition*, Oktober 23, 1933, p. 3. In another review, Auerbach emphasizes both wall pictures, one abstract and one figurative, that were integrated in the architecture and the exhibition.

43 In January 1933, Kiesler met several representatives of major furniture manufacturers, for example from Baker Furniture Inc., for whom the American designer Donald Deskey worked, and from Kroehler Furniture. In the now improved economic conditions, Kiesler sees good chance of obtaining contracts as a product designer.
The literature indicates various first names and various spellings of the surname as Mergentine and Mergentime.
The name given in the *AUDAC* brochure is Marguerita Mergentime.

44 Letter from Frederick Kiesler to Steffi Kiesler, undated, Archive of the Kiesler Foundation Vienna.

45 Cf. *AUDAC* brochure, Archive of the Kiesler Foundation Vienna.

46 Steffi Kiesler notes down a meeting on July 28 of Kiesler, Sidney Janis and Marguerite Mergentime; on December 21, Steffi writes, "Abendessen zu Mergentime to look over Apartment (nobody there)," Steffi Kiesler's calendar, 1935, Archive of the Kiesler Foundation Vienna.

47 Steffi Kiesler's calendar entries of 1936, Archive of the Kiesler Foundation Vienna.

48 Kiesler's patent filing for the *Party Lounge* is registered on January 24, 1936. A number of changes made by Kiesler, formal corrections and bureaucratic obstacles placed by the Patent Office delay confirmation of the patent. The patent is finally handed over to Kiesler on August 23, 1939.

30 Entwurf für das Möbelensemble für Mergentime,
    New York ca. 1933.
    Sketch for furniture for Mergentime,
    New York c. 1933.

31 Blick in die Wohnung von Charles und Marguerite
    Mergentime mit dem Lamp Table (Mitte),
    Bed Couch (rechts), Tisch (vorne), zwei Teile eines
    Nesting Coffee Table (links und rechts) und einem
    Bücherregal (links) von Friedrich Kiesler.
    View into the apartment of Charles and
    Marguerite Mergentime with the *Lamp Table*
    (center), *Bed Couch* (right), a glass table (fore-
    ground), two pieces of a *Nesting Coffee Table*
    (left and right) and a bookshelf (left) by
    Frederick Kiesler.

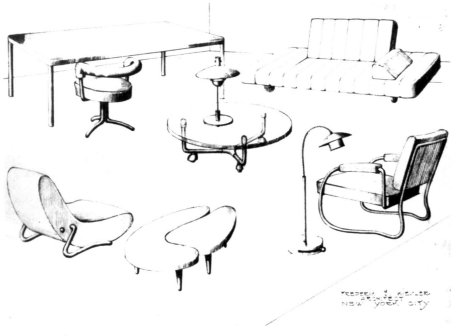

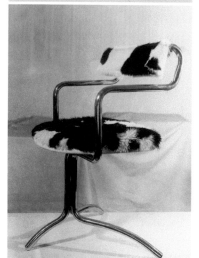

AUDAC.[45] Erst im Sommer 1935 gelangen die Entwürfe zur Ausführung.[46] (Abb. 31) Nelson Rockefeller lässt zu jener Zeit sein Apartment von Wallace K. Harrison, ebenfalls einem *AUDAC*-Mitglied und Freund Friedrich Kieslers, umbauen. Der gemeinsame Besuch der Wohnung Mergentime mit dem Architekten Philip Johnson und Rockefeller Jr. soll Kiesler der Bewerbung seines eigenen Möbeldesigns dienen.[47] Es ist anzunehmen, dass er zu jener Zeit mit weiteren Aufträgen rechnet. Anfang 1936 reicht er Patente für verschiedene Möbel des Ensembles ein, darunter die *Party Lounge*.[48] (Abb. 32)

Es entstehen zahlreiche Entwürfe und Studien zu den verschiedenen Möbeln des Wohnzimmers. Zwei *Nesting Coffee Tables*, (Abb. 33) eine Herren- und eine Damenkommode, ein Tisch mit sechs Sesseln (Abb. 34, 35), der sogenannte *Lamp Table*, die *Bed Couch* (Abb. 36-47) und die *Party Lounge* (Abb. 48-68). Dazu ein Sofasessel und ein Freischwinger, die jedoch nicht zur Ausführung kommen. (Abb. 30) Kiesler führt sein modernes Design konsequent aus den ersten Realisierungen eines Büroraums fort. Stahlrohr, Glas und Metall kombiniert mit lackiertem Markassa-Holz und verschiedenen Polsterungen aus farbigem Kunstleder bestimmen das Design. Merkmale dieser Ensembles bleiben Multifunktionalität, Flexibilität und Veränderlichkeit der einzelnen Elemente, sowie ihre variablen Kombinationsmöglichkeiten. Die *Bed Couch* wird zur Liege, die *Party Lounge* zu einem Bett und der dreiteilige und zweiteilige *Nesting Coffee Table* ist in seinen Einzelteilen jeweils mit den anderen Möbeln als Couchtisch, Beistelltisch oder Nachttisch kombinierbar. Einige Möbel, wie der *Lamp Table* und die Sofas sind mit Rollen versehen und in ihrer Positionierung leicht zu verändern. Die organischen Formen der *Nesting Coffee Tables* stellen ausgehend vom *Space House* eine wegweisende Entwicklung in Kieslers Design dar. Sie entstehen gemeinsam mit den ersten theoretischen Texten zur „DesignCorrelation". Ein Begriff den Kiesler in der Folge zu einer umfassenden künstlerisch-wissenschaftlichen Gestalttheorie ausbaut und der für seine Ausstellungsgestaltungen der 40er Jahre, sowie für die Architekturentwürfe des *Endless House* der 50er Jahre prägend werden soll.

45 Siehe Broschüre *AUDAC*, Archiv der Kiesler Stiftung Wien.

46 Steffi Kiesler verzeichnet ein Treffen am 28. Juli zwischen Kiesler, Sidney Janis und Marguerite Mergentime, am 21. Dezember vermerkt Steffi: „Abendessen zu Mergentime to look over Apartment (nobody there)", Kalender Steffi Kiesler, Jahr 1935, Archiv der Kiesler Stiftung Wien.

47 Kalendereinträge Steffi Kieslers von 1936, Archiv der Kiesler Stiftung Wien.

48 Am 24. Januar 1936 kommt es zur Registrierung der Einreichung von Kieslers Patent für die *Party Lounge*. Verschiedene inhaltliche Veränderungen von Seiten Kieslers, formale Korrekturen und bürokratische Hürden von Seiten des Patentamts, verzögern die Bestätigung des Patents. Am 23. August 1939 wird Kiesler das Patent schließlich ausgehändigt.

Kiesler created numerous plans and studies for the various sitting-room furnishings. Two *Nesting Coffee Tables*, (Fig. 33) a men's and women's chest of drawers, a table with six chairs, (Fig. 34, 35) the *Lamp Table*, the *Bed Couch*, (Fig. 36-47) and the *Party Lounge*. (Fig. 48-68) In addition, a sofa chair and a cantilever chair, which were, however, not actually built. (Fig. 30) Kiesler continued to develop his modern design on the basis of his first office interiors. The design is characterized by steel tubing, glass and metal combined with varnished Macassar wood and various upholsteries of colored leather. The distinctive features of these sets are still multifunctionality, flexibility and variability of the separate elements, as well as variable combination options. The *Bed Couch* turns into a lounger, the *Party Lounge* turns into a bed, and the various parts of the three-part and two-part *Nesting Coffee Table* can be combined with other pieces of furniture to make a couch table, side-table or bedside table. Some pieces of furniture such as the *Lamp Table* and sofas are on castors and easy to move around. Based on the *Space House*, the organic forms of the *Nesting Coffee Tables* constitute a pioneering development in Kiesler's design. They were created at the same time as his first theoretical writings on *Design-Correlation*. A concept that Kiesler subsequently developed to refer to a comprehensive artistic, scientific theory of design and that was to be characteristic of his exhibition designs in the nineteen-forties and for the architectural designs for the *Endless House* in the fifties.

Bed Couch

Ursprünglich war die *Bed Couch* mit abgestepptem Kunstleder bezogen. Über die Farbigkeit des Bezugs sind uns widersprüchliche Angaben überliefert. Ähnlich der *Party Lounge* liegen die gepolsterte Sitzfläche und Rückenlehne auf einem durchlaufenden Stahlrohrgestell auf. Der Rahmen läuft über die Seiten nach oben und bildet die Armstützen aus. Diese dienen auch zur Arretierung der Lehne. Die Couch ist durch einen Klappmechanismus in ein Bett verwandelbar. Die beiden variablen Elemente sind von unterschiedlicher Tiefe, daher ergibt sich bei diesem Möbel eine dreifache Nutzung. Wegen der unterschiedlichen Tiefen der verstellbaren Elemente muss in die Unterkonstruktion ein zusätzliches Paar Rollen integriert werden.

The *Bed Couch* was originally covered with quilted artificial leather. There are contradictory records of the color of the upholstery. Similar to the *Party Lounge*, the cushioned seat and backrest rest on a continuous steel-tube frame. The frame turns up at the sides, thus forming the armrests, that are also used to lock the backrest. The couch can be converted into a bed with a snap mechanism. Both variable elements vary in depth, thus allowing the lounge to be used for three different purposes. Due to the different depths of the variable elements, an additional pair of castors must be integrated into the substructure.

36   *Bed Couch*, Prototyp, 1935-36,

Privatsammlung.

Bed Couch, prototype, 1935-36,

Private Collection.

37-39   Studie für ein Sofa, ca. 1933-39.

Study for a couch, c. 1933-39.

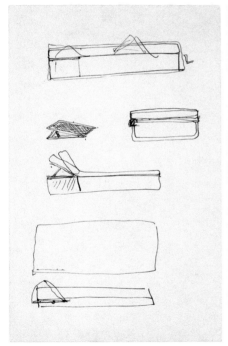

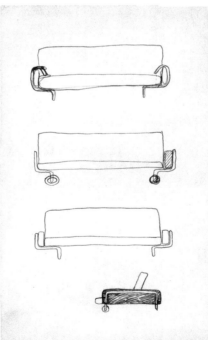

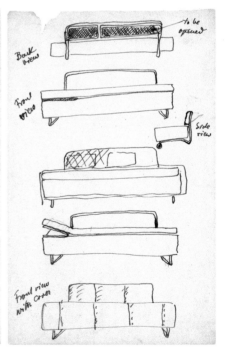

37   38   39

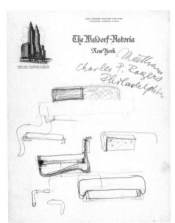

40

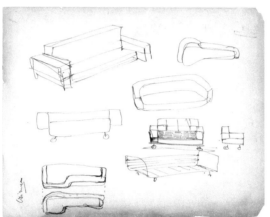

41

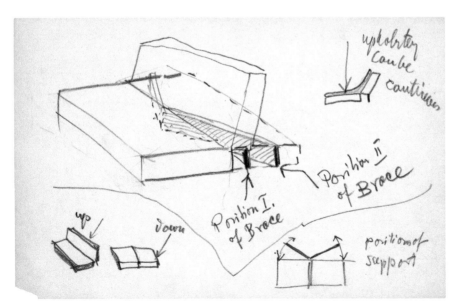

42

44

44   *Bed Couch*, Prototyp, 1935-39,

      Privatsammlung.

      Bed Couch, prototype, 1935-39,

      Private Collection.

45-47   Studie zur *Bed Couch*, ca. 1933-39.

       Study for *Bed Couch*, c. 1933-39.

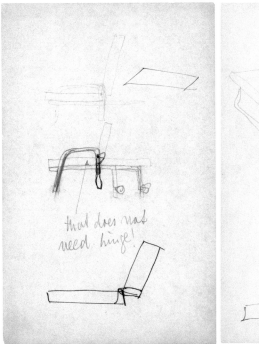

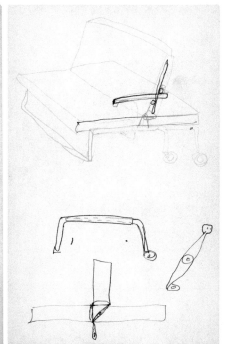

45

46

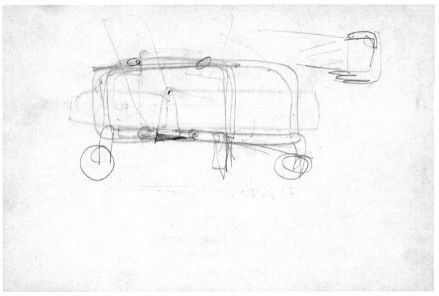

47

Party Lounge

Ein Stahlrohrgestell bildet den Rahmen und trägt die gepolsterte Sitzfläche. Ein Teil der Liegefläche ist nach oben hin verstellbar, das Kunstleder (Naugahyde) abgesteppt. Die *Party Lounge* steht auf Rollen deren Mechanismus durch das Gewicht der Personen arretiert. Nicht in Gebrauch bleibt das Möbel beweglich. Durch Aufklappen eines Teils des Sofas erscheint das Möbel nicht nur größer, sondern ermöglicht auch mehreren Leuten verschiedene Sitzpositionen. Für die *Party Lounge* entstehen zahlreiche Skizzen und Studien. Die Möglichkeit zur Umfunktionierung von einer Couch zu einem Bett ist bereits in den ersten Zeichnungen angelegt. Kiesler experimentiert in der Folge mit verschiedenen Aufsätzen und Schiebemechanismen zur Erweiterung der Nutzung seiner *Party Lounge*.

A steel-tube frame forms the basic structure carrying the cushioned seat. Part of the reclining surface can be raised, the artificial leather (Naugahyde) quilted. The *Party Lounge* stands on castors, whose mechanism locks under the weight of the sitters. The piece of furniture is movable when not in use. Folding out part of the sofa not only causes the lounge to appear larger, but also provides different seating positions for several people. Numerous sketches and studies were done for the *Party Lounge*. The option of transforming the couch into a bed is already indicated in the first drawings. Kiesler subsequently experiments with various upper parts and sliding mechanisms to increase the number of uses for his *Party Lounge*.

48   *Party Lounge*, Prototyp, 1935-36,

Sammlung Evan Janis, New York.

Foto: Joshua Nefsky.

Party Lounge, prototype, 1935-36,

Collection Evan Janis, New York.

Photograph by Joshua Nefsky.

49   Studie für ein Sofa, ca. 1933-39.

Study for a couch, c. 1933-39.

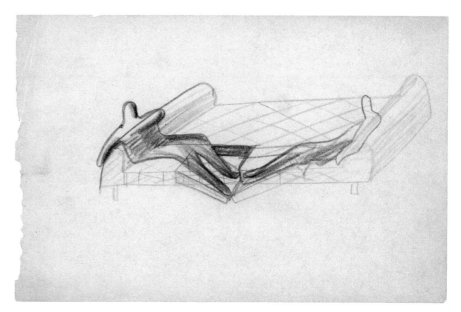

49

50   *Party Lounge*, Prototyp, 1935-36,

Sammlung Evan Janis, New York.

Foto: Joshua Nefsky.

Party Lounge, prototype, 1935-36,

Collection Evan Janis, New York.

Photograph by Joshua Nefsky.

51-52   Studie zur *Party Lounge*, ca. 1933-39.

Study for *Party Lounge*, c. 1933-39.

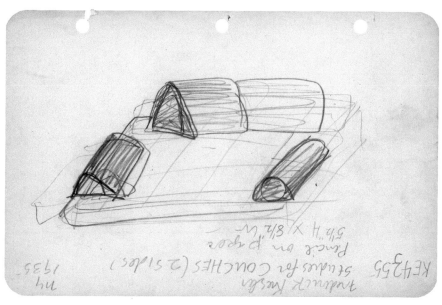

51

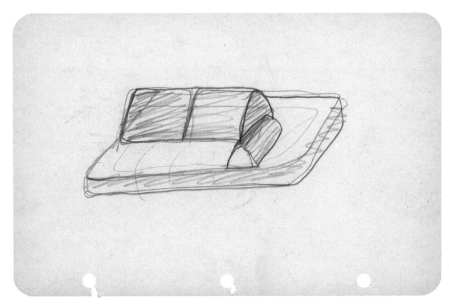

52

53

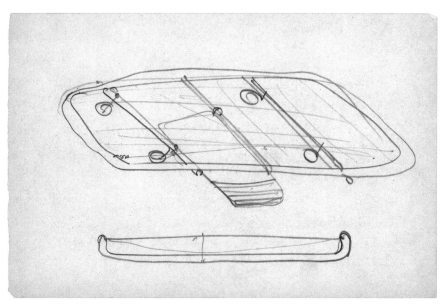

54

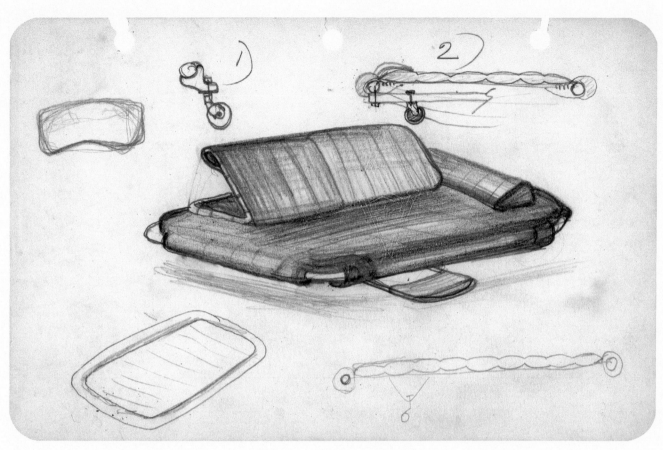

56

56   Studie zur *Party Lounge*, ca. 1933-39.

Study for *Party Lounge*, c. 1933-39.

57-58   Studien für ein klappbares Sofa,

New York 1937-41.

Studies for a convertible couch,

New York 1937-41.

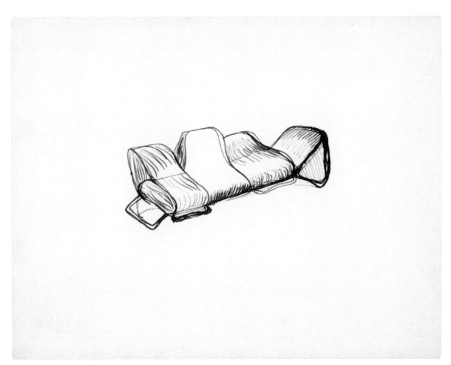

57

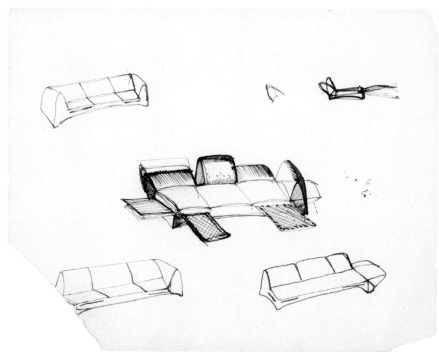

58

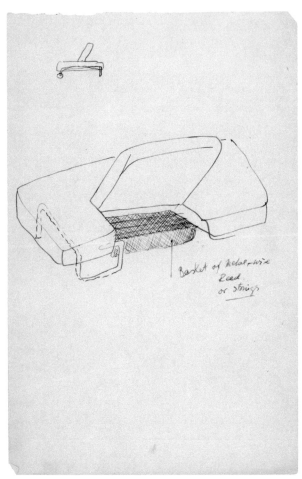

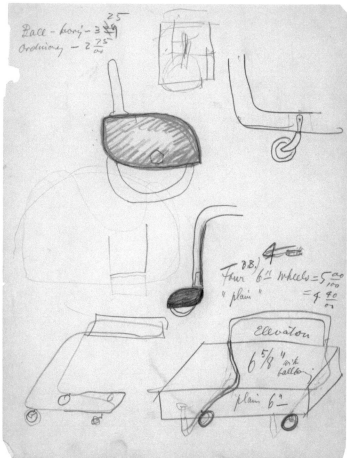

59

60

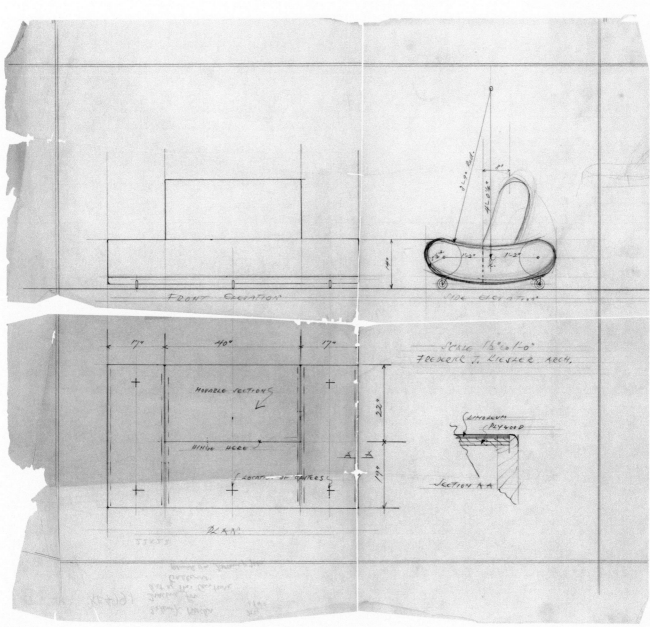

FRONT ELEVATION

SIDE ELEVATION

3'-9" Rad.

8"

4'-0½"

1'-2"

1'-2"

14"

17"   40"   17"

MOVABLE SECTIONS

HINGE HERE

LOCATION OF CASTERS

PLAN

A A

22"

19"

SCALE 1½"=1'-0"

FREDERICK J. KIESLER, ARCH.

LINOLEUM

PLYWOOD

SECTION A-A

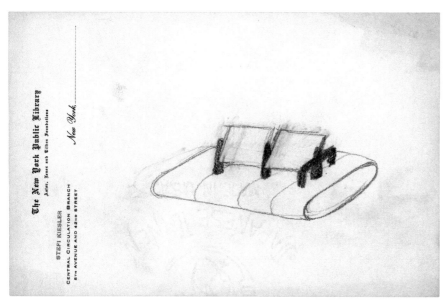

64

64   *Party Lounge*, Prototyp, 1935-36,

     Sammlung Evan Janis, New York.

     Foto: Joshua Nefsky.

     Party Lounge, prototype, 1935-36,

     Collection Evan Janis, New York.

     Photograph by Joshua Nefsky.

65   Entwurf für ein Sofa, ca. 1939-41.

     Sketch for a couch, c. 1939-41.

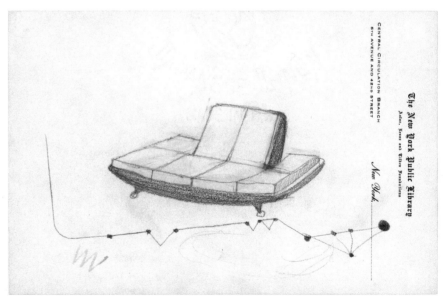

65

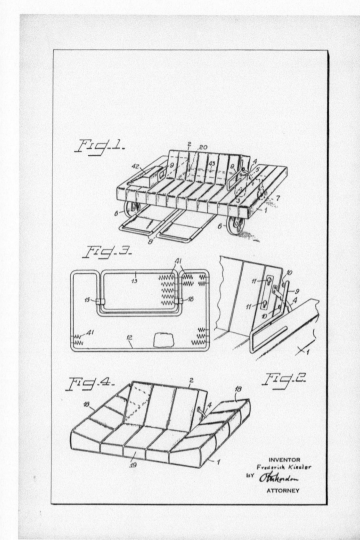

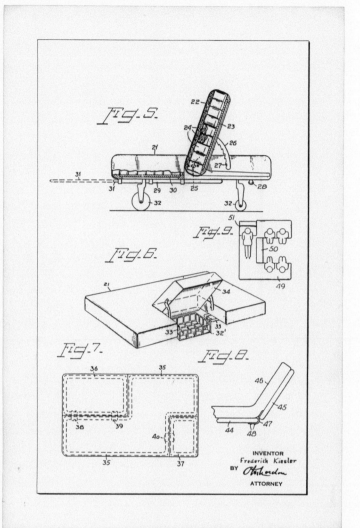

Von der *Clinic of Modern Design* zum *Laboratory for Design Correlation*

Im Design vollzieht sich um 1933 ein entscheidender Formwandel. Streng geometrische Formen weichen gestalterischen Ansätzen einer organischen Formensprache. Mit dem Schlagwort des „biomorphen Design" werden die Entwicklungen, wie etwa in Alvar Aaltos, Marcel Breuers oder Bruno Mathssons Entwürfen betitelt.[49]

In den Möbeln für die Wohnung Mergentime zeichnet sich ebenfalls eine Orientierung zu einer runderen Gestaltung ab. Zur selben Zeit beginnt sich Kiesler auch verstärkt mit theoretischen Fragestellungen zu Architektur und Design auseinander zu setzen. *Architectural Record* veröffentlicht in den 30er Jahren zahlreiche Schriften zu seinen Thesen. Nach der Konsolidierung amerikanischen Industriedesigns nimmt Kiesler eine Tendenz in der Produktgestaltung wahr, die er als technokratische Bewegung bezeichnet. Technisch-wirtschaftliche Fragen würden nach Kiesler mehr denn je den gestalterischen Problemlösungen übergeordnet. In seiner Textserie „Design-Correlation"[50] geht es vor allem um die Etablierung einer progressiven „Wissenschaft der Gestaltung" durch intensives Studium der Zusammenhänge zwischen den Künsten, der Technik und der natürlichen Umgebung.

Ein Auslöser für Kieslers verstärkte Hinwendung zur Theorie stellt die „Modern Architecture: International Exhibition" 1932, bekannt geworden unter dem Schlagwort „International Style" im Museum of Modern Art in New York dar. Zahlreiche Modelle und Entwürfe von mehrheitlich europäischen Architekten der Avantgarde, wie etwa Walter Gropius, Ludwig Mies van der Rohe und Le Corbusier werden dort gezeigt. Kiesler ist mit seiner Gestaltung des *Film Guild Cinema* in der Schau vertreten. Die Kritik amerikanischer Architekten und Theoretiker richtet sich gegen die durch das Ausstellungskonzept zu rein stilisierten Architekturformeln simplifizierten Gestaltprozesse der Moderne.[51] Auch wird moniert, dass die Hinwendung zu einer funktionalistischen Architekturauffassung die Auseinandersetzung mit der Architektur im eigenen Land ausblende und der theoretische Diskurs, darunter die Texte von Frank Lloyd Wright zu einer organischen Architektur nicht berücksichtigt werden.

Gleichzeitig verkörpert Ludwig Mies van der Rohe als letzter Bauhausdirektor in Berlin die Architektur-Avantgarde zu jener Zeit in Amerika. 1934 publiziert E. M. Benson den Text „Wanted: An American Institute for Industrial Design."[52] Darin publiziert Kiesler erste Architekturentwürfe für ein derartiges Institut, dessen Programm sich explizit auf das deutsche Bauhaus als Vorbild bezieht. Kiesler selbst meldet den Bedarf an einer progressiven Kunstschule an und versucht noch vor der Ankunft der Bauhaus-Vertreter in Amerika um 1937 ein Institut in Anleh-

49 Siehe dazu: Lisa Philips, *High Styles; Twentieth-Century American Design*, New York 1985, und Paul Johnson, Design 1935-1965, *What Modern Was*, New York 1991.

50 Insgesamt erscheinen 5 Texte in dieser Serie zwischen 1937 und 1939 in *Architectural Record*, siehe dazu Literaturliste im Anhang.

51 In der Architekturzeitschrift *Shelter* erscheint 1932 ein Bericht des Symposiums zur Ausstellung International Style, mit Artikeln von Frank Lloyd Wright, Harvey Leslie Corbett, Eugene Schoen. Zur Rolle der Zeitschriften im Architekturdiskurs der 30er Jahre, siehe Hyungmin Pai, *The Portfolio and the Diagram*, New York 2002.

52 E. M. Benson, „Wanted: An American Institute for Industrial Design", in: *The American Magazine of Art*, Juni 1934.

From the *Clinic of Modern Design* to the *Laboratory for Design Correlation*

Design underwent a decisive change of form around 1933. Strictly geometric forms gave way to the design approaches of an organic vocabulary of form. The buzzword "biomorphic design" came to refer to these developments, for example as seen in the designs of Alvar Aalto, Marcel Breuer or Bruno Mathsson.[49]

A gradual changeover to rounder shapes can also be observed in the furniture for the Mergentime apartment. At the same time, Kiesler also began to deal increasingly with theoretical questions of architecture and design. The *Architectural Record* published numerous articles on his theories in the thirties. Following the consolidation of American industrial design, Kiesler perceived a trend in product design that he described as a technocratic movement. More than ever, according to Kiesler, technical and economic issues were being given greater priority over design solutions. His series of texts on "Design Correlation"[50] focused above all on establishing a progressive "science of design" by scrutinizing the correlations between the arts, technology and the natural environment.

One thing that induced Kiesler to concentrate more strongly on aspects of theory was the "Modern Architecture: International Exhibition" of 1932, which became known by the catchword "International Style," at the Museum of Modern Art in New York. The show featured numerous models and designs by primarily European avant-garde architects such as Walter Gropius, Ludwig Mies van der Rohe and Le Corbusier. Kiesler took part in the show with his design for the *Film Guild Cinema*. The criticism of American architects and theorists was aimed at the design processes of modernism that were simplified in the exhibition concept as purely stylized architectural formulas.[51] They also complained that the changeover to a functionalistic conception of architecture failed to focus on the architectural discussion in the country and disregarded the theoretical debate, including the writings of Frank Lloyd Wright on organic architecture.

At the same time, Ludwig Mies van der Rohe, the last director of the Bauhaus in Berlin, embodied the avant-garde in architecture in America at the time. E. M. Benson published "Wanted: An American Institute for Industrial Design"[52] in 1934, in which Kiesler published his first architectural plans for such an institute, whose program was styled explicitly on the German Bauhaus. Kiesler himself indicated the need for a progressive art school and, even before the arrival of representatives of the Bauhaus in America around 1937, attempted to found an institute based on their program.[53] Kiesler's early teaching ambi-

49   Cf.: Lisa Philips, *High Styles; Twentieth-Century American Design*, New York 1985, and Paul Johnson, Design 1935-1965, *What Modern Was*, New York 1991.

50   A total of five texts were published in this series between 1937 and 1939 in *Architectural Record*, cf. list of literature in the appendix.

51   In 1932, the architecture magazine *Shelter* published a report of the symposium on the International Style exhibition, with articles by Frank Lloyd Wright, Harvey Leslie Corbett, and Eugene Schoen. On the role of magazines in the architectural discourse of the thirties cf. Hyungmin Pai, *The Portfolio and the Diagram*, New York 2002.

52   E. M. Benson, "Wanted: An American Institute for Industrial Design", in: *The American Magazine of Art*, June 1934.

53   On the reception of the Bauhaus in America after 1933 cf. Margret Kentgens-Craig, *Bauhaus & America: First Contacts, 1919-1936*, New York 2001.

nung an deren Programm zu etablieren.[53] Mit der Gründung seines *Laboratory for Design Correlation* an der School of Architecture der Columbia University nehmen Kieslers frühe Ambitionen auf eine Lehrtätigkeit endlich Gestalt an.[54] Sein Plädoyer für intensive wissenschaftliche Auseinandersetzung auf interdisziplinärer Basis stellt sich dabei gegen die Forderung nach schnellen Ergebnissen, die allein modische Trends schaffen. „Einer der beunruhigendsten Faktoren in der Design-Ausbildung ist das Verlangen nach einer schnellen Adaptierung von neuen Schemata." Polemisch heißt es weiter: „Ein typisches Beispiel dafür ist die von heute auf morgen erfolgte Einrichtung einer Bauhaus-Imitation in Chicago und von weiteren Bauhaus-Imitationen im ganzen Land."[55]

Mies van der Rohe kommt 1937 nach Amerika und trifft Kiesler mehrmals in dessen Penthouse in der 57sten Straße. (Abb. 69) Zu jener Zeit lehrt Kiesler bereits an der Columbia University und ist daher auch in der Lage, Mies über die Rezeption dessen Arbeit in Amerika zu informieren. Kiesler und Mies achten einander und bleiben sich zu Lebzeiten freundschaftlich verbunden, sie verfolgen jedoch völlig unterschiedliche Lehransätze. Kiesler rückt den sozial interagierenden Menschen und dessen Verhalten, seine Wünsche und Bedürfnisse in den Mittelpunkt seiner gestalterischen Überlegung, wogegen Mies die „Klärung der ordnenden Prinzipien" ins Zentrum stellt, um darauf basierend die „systematische Struktur zu einer organischen Entfaltung von spirituellen und kulturellen Beziehungen"[56] gestalterisch umzusetzen. Kiesler steht in Bezug auf die Lehre eher Mies' Bauhauskollegen László Moholy-Nagy nahe, welcher 1937 das New Bauhaus in Chicago gründet.[57] Er ist es auch, der Kiesler 1944 mehrmals einlädt, Vorträge über die Design-Theorie des *Correalismus* zu halten.

Die zentrale Schrift zur Erklärung seiner umfassenden Gestalttheorie „On Correalism and Biotechnique, Definition and Test of a New Approach to Building Design" erscheint während seiner Tätigkeit am *Laboratory for Design Correlation* im September 1939.[58] In den naturwissenschaftlichen Erkenntnissen des Elektromagnetismus und der Gravitationslehre sieht Kiesler die grundsätzlichen energetischen Muster von trennenden und integrierenden Kräften bestätigt, die unser menschliches Leben beeinflussen. „Das sichtbare Ergebnis dieser aktivierenden Kräfte wird üblicherweise als *Materie* bezeichnet, sie bildet das, was wir im allgemeinen als Realität verstehen."[59] Zudem existieren aber noch unsichtbare Kräfte, die der Mensch nur bedingt wahrnehmen könne, da das Vermögen seiner sinnlichen Wahrnehmung limitiert sei. Form konstituiert sich für Kiesler demnach durch ein sichtbares und unsichtbares Wechselspiel von Kräften, das einer ständigen Veränderung unterliegt.[60] „Den Austausch interagierender Kräfte bezeichne ich als CO-REALITÄT und die Wissenschaft von den Gesetzen dieser Wechselbezie-

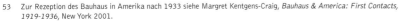

53   Zur Rezeption des Bauhaus in Amerika nach 1933 siehe Margret Kentgens-Craig, *Bauhaus & America: First Contacts, 1919-1936*, New York 2001.

54   Kiesler schreibt an seine Frau 1933: „Ich hoffe meine Bemühungen werden wenigstens universitäre Früchte tragen." Brief von Friedrich Kiesler an seine Frau Steffi am 11. Januar 1933, Archiv der Kiesler Stiftung Wien.

55   Frederick Kiesler, *First Report on Laboratory for Design Correlation*, undatiert (um 1938), Archiv der Kiesler Stiftung Wien.

56   Phyllis Lambert, *Mies van der Rohe in America*, New York 2004, S. 182.

57   Kentgens-Craig, 2001 (wie Anm. 55).

58   Frederick Kiesler, „On Correalism and Biotechnique. A Definition and Test of a New Approach to Building Design", in: *Architectural Record*, 86/3, September 1939.

59   Ebd. S. 61.

60   Ebd. S. 62.

69 Mies van der Rohe (rechts) mit unbekannter

Person auf Kieslers Terrasse, 1937.

Mies van der Rohe (right) and an unidentified man

on Kiesler's terrace, 1937.

70 Kiesler mit seinem Metabolism Chart, ca. 1947.

Kiesler and his Metabolism Chart, c. 1947.

71 *Mobile Home Library*, Fotomontage,

publiziert in: *Architectural Record*, 1939.

Foto: Ezra Stoller.

Mobile Home Library, photomontage,

published in: *Architectural Record*, 1939.

Photograph by Ezra Stoller.

tions finally materialized with the foundation of his *Laboratory for Design Correlation* at the School of Architecture of Columbia University.[54] In this context, his plea for an in-depth interdisciplinary scientific analysis was in opposition to demands for fast results, that only fashionable trends can produce. "One of the most disturbing factors in design-education is the desire for quick adaption of new formulas." He continued polemically, "A typical example of that is the overnight establishement of an imitation Bauhaus in Chicago and other imitation Bauhauses throughout the country."[55]

Mies van der Rohe came to America in 1937, where he met Kiesler at his Penthouse on 57th Street several times. (Fig. 69) At this time, Kiesler was already teaching at Columbia University and was therefore in a position to inform Mies about the reception of his work in America. Kiesler and Mies respected each other and remained on friendly terms throughout their lives, although they each took completely different approaches to teaching. While Kiesler focused on man as a social interactor and his behavior, his wishes and needs in his consideration of design, Mies centered on "clarifying the ordering principles" so as to translate their "systematic structure" into design "in order to permit an organic development of spiritual and cultural relationships"[56] on this basis. With regard to teaching, Kiesler was in fact closer to Mies's Bauhaus colleague László Moholy-Nagy, who founded the New Bauhaus in Chicago in 1937.[57] It was he who invited Kiesler to hold lectures about the *Correalism* design theory on several occasions in 1944.

The main treatise explaining his comprehensive design theory "On Correalism and Biotechnique, Definition and Test of a New Approach to Building Design" was published during his work at the *Laboratory for Design Correlation* in September 1939.[58] Kiesler saw the fundamental energetic patterns of divisive and integrating forces that influence human life confirmed by the findings of natural science in the fields of electromagnetism and gravitation. "The visible result of these activating forces is usually called *matter* and consists what is commonly understood as reality."[59] But, he maintained, there also exist invisible forces that humans can only perceive to a certain extent, their capacity of sensory perception being limited. For Kiesler, then, form is constituted by a visible and invisible interplay of forces that is subject to constant change.[60] "The exchange of interacting forces I call CO-REALITY, and the Science of the laws of interrelationships, CORREALISM. The Term <correalism> expresses the dynamics of the continual interaction between man and his natural and technological environment."[61] Kiesler's holistic approach to design, based upon physical, physiological and psychological principles, contrasts

69

54   Kiesler writes to his wife in 1933, "I hope my efforts will at least bear fruits at the universities." Letter from
     Frederick Kiesler to his wife Steffi on January 11, 1933, Archive of the Kiesler Foundation Vienna.
55   Frederick Kiesler, *First Report on Laboratory for Design Correlation*, undated (c. 1938), Archive of the
     Kiesler Foundation Vienna.
56   Phyllis Lambert, *Mies van der Rohe in America*, New York 2004, p. 182.
57   Kentgens-Craig, 2001 (cf. note 55).
58   Frederick Kiesler, "On Correalism and Biotechnique. A Definition and Test of a New Approach to Building Design",
     in: *Architectural Record*, 86/3, September 1939.
59   Op. cit. p. 61.
60   Op. cit. p. 62.
61   Op. cit.

hungen als CORREALISMUS. Der Ausdruck <Correalismus> bringt die Dynamik der fortlaufenden Wechselwirkungen zwischen dem Menschen und seiner natürlichen und technischen Umgebung zum Ausdruck."[61] Kieslers ganzheitlicher Gestaltungsansatz nach physikalischen, physiologischen und psychologischen Grundsätzen setzt sich deutlich von den Theorien des Bauhaus ab. Als Beispiel dient Kiesler die Konstruktion eines Bücherregals, die *Mobile Home Library*, welche in seinem Laboratory um 1939 entsteht. (Abb. 71) Die Interaktion der Kräfte zwischen dem Benutzer und dem Möbel werden genau analysiert und in einem „Metabolism Chart" festgehalten. (Abb. 70) Aus dem Studium der Gegebenheiten und ihrer Verhältnisse wird die formale Umsetzung abgeleitet. Resultat ist in diesem Fall ein im Ganzen und in den einzelnen Teilen drehbares Möbel zur Schaffung möglichst vielseitiger Funktionen.

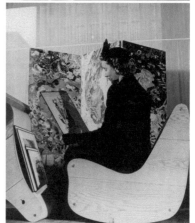

Ausstellungsgestaltungen der 40er Jahre

Das *Laboratory for Design Correlation* wird 1941 nach vierjähriger Tätigkeit geschlossen. Kiesler lässt sich den Begriff *Correalismus* 1938 offiziell schützen.[62] Die Ergebnisse seiner Auseinandersetzung mit Architektur- und Designtheorie des letzten Jahrzehnts fließen nun in die Umsetzung der revolutionären Inneneinrichtung für Peggy Guggenheims neue Galerie *Art of This Century* in New York ein.[63]

Im Zuge seiner umfassenden Ausstellungsgestaltung entstehen fünf verschiedene Sitzgelegenheiten. Zwei Varianten eines Regiestuhls, mit und ohne Lehne, (Abb. 72, 73) das *Correalistische Instrument* in zwei Versionen und der *Correalistische Rocker*. (Abb. 74, 91) In den ersten Materiallisten ist von 90 Sesseln die Rede. Tatsächlich werden nur 30 Stück ausgeführt.[64] Über die Gründe der ursprünglich hohen Stückzahl lässt sich nur spekulieren. Wahrscheinlich versucht Kiesler im Rahmen dieses Auftrags die Finanzierung einer höheren Auflage zu sichern. Über den Produktionsprozess schreibt Kiesler: „[...] die ganze Konstruktion wurde in kleinen Werkstätten im Raum New York ausgearbeitet, deren entschiedene Hilfe bei der tatsächlichen Umsetzung in diesen schwierigen Zeiten oft soweit ging, dass eigene finanzielle Interessen geopfert wurden."[65] Später erinnert er sich: „Die multifunktionellen Sessel habe ich selbst mit Hilfe eines deutschen Tischlers in einer Garage in der Bronx gebaut."[66] Die erschwerte Arbeitssituation in New York, bedingt durch den Kriegseintritt 1941 und den damit zusammenhängenden wirtschaftlichen Verschlechterungen, trifft vor allem kleine Firmen und Handwerksbetriebe. Materialrestriktionen, sowie Preis- und Produktionsvorgaben verschärfen die Situation auch für Möbeldesigner.[67]

61   Ebd.
62   Bestätigung zum Eintrag im Washington Patent Office 1938, Archiv der Kiesler Stiftung Wien.
63   Brief von Peggy Guggenheim an Friedrich Kiesler, 26.2.1942, Archiv der Kiesler Stiftung Wien.
64   Siehe die genauen Ausführungen und Inventarliste zu den Möbeln der Galerie, Don Quaintance, „Modern Art in a Modern Setting", in: *Peggy Guggenheim & Frederick Kiesler. The Story of Art of This Century*, S. 240-249.
65   *Press Release Pertaining to the Architectural Aspects of the Gallery*, Typskript 1942, Archiv der Kiesler Stiftung Wien. (Orig. Zit. in Engl.)
66   Creighton 1961, (wie Anm. 2), S. 116.
67   Wirtschaftliche Maßnahmen durch das Office of Production Management (OPM), dem späteren War Production Board und dem Office of Price Administration (OPA) haben direkte Auswirkungen auf die Möbelproduktion. Siehe dazu: David M. Kennedy, *Freedom from Fear*, New York 2001.

72   Detail eines Klappstuhls in der Daylight Gallery,

Art of This Century, New York 1942.

Foto: Berenice Abbott.

Detail of a folding chair in the Daylight Gallery,

Art of This Century, New York 1942.

Photograph by Berenice Abbott.

73   Peggy Guggenheim auf einem Klappstuhl in

der Daylight Gallery, *Art of This Century,*

New York 1942. Courtesy Solomon

R. Guggenheim Foundation, New York.

Foto: Berenice Abbott.

Peggy Guggenheim sitting on a folding chair

in the Daylight Gallery, *Art of This Century,*

New York 1942. Courtesy Solomon

R. Guggenheim Foundation, New York.

Photograph by Berenice Abbott.

74   Unbekannte Person auf einem

Correalistischen Rocker in der Daylight Gallery,

Art of This Century, New York 1942.

Foto: Berenice Abbott.

Unidentified woman sitting on a

Correalist Rocker in the Daylight Gallery,

Art of This Century, New York 1942.

Photograph by Berenice Abbott.

distinctly with the theories of the Bauhaus. As an example, Kiesler used the design of a bookshelf, the *Mobile Home Library*, designed in his laboratory around 1939. (Fig. 71) He analyzed the interaction of forces between the user and the piece of furniture in great detail, recording them in a "Metabolism Chart". (Fig. 70) By studying the conditions and their interrelations, he derived the formal realization. In this case, the result is an item of furniture that may be swiveled as a whole and its individual components, designed to allow a wide range of uses.

Exhibition Designs in the Forties

The *Laboratory for Design Correlation* was closed in 1941 after four years in operation. Kiesler had the term *Correalism* officially protected in 1938.[62] The results of his analysis of the theory of architecture and design over the previous decade were now incorporated into the revolutionary interior design for Peggy Guggenheim's new gallery *Art of This Century* in New York.[63]

He designed five different seats in the course of his comprehensive exhibition design. Two variations on a director's chair, with and without a backrest, (Fig. 72, 73) two versions of the *Correalist Instrument*, and the *Correalist Rocker*. (Fig. 74, 91) The first material lists indicated ninety chairs. Only thirty were actually built.[64] We can only speculate on the large number originally planned. Kiesler probably tried to use this contract to obtain funding for a larger number. Kiesler wrote of the production process, "[...] all the construction has been worked out in small shops·in the New York area, with their distinct help to carry through the actual remodeling in these difficult times to the point of often sacrificing their own financial profits."[65] Later he recalled, "The chairs of many functions I constructed myself with the help of a German carpenter in a garage in the Bronx."[66] The compounded working situation in New York, due to America joining the war in 1941 and the contingent worsening of the economic situation, above all affected small companies and workshops. Material restrictions, along with regulations concerning pricing and production, also aggravated the situation for furniture designers.[67]

The entire theory of free tensions in space and of the relation between the user and a piece of furniture was manifested in the *Correalist Instrument.* Kiesler later described the process as follows, "The two-seat rest-form also grew from the principle of continuous tension. I took a form similar to a wave, and curved in such a way as to create an object with no beginning and no end;

62   Confirmation of registration at the Washington Patent Office in 1938, Archive of the Kiesler Foundation Vienna.

63   Letter from Peggy Guggenheim to Frederick Kiesler, February 26, 1942, Archive of the Kiesler Foundation Vienna.

64   Cf. the detailed explanations and furniture inventory of the gallery, Don Quaintance, "Modern Art in a Modern Setting", in: *Peggy Guggenheim & Frederick Kiesler. The Story of Art of This Century,* p. 240-249.

65   *Press Release Pertaining to the Architectural Aspects of the Gallery,* typescript 1942, Archive of the Kiesler Foundation Vienna.

66   Creighton 1961, (cf. note 2), p. 116.

67   Economic measures enacted by the Office of Production Management (OPM), the later War Production Board and the Office of Price Administration (OPA) impacted directly on furniture production. Cf.: David M. Kennedy, *Freedom from Fear,* New York 2001.

In dem *Correalistischen Instrument* manifestiert sich die gesamte Theorie der freien Spannungen im Raum und der Relation zwischen dem Benutzer und einem Möbel. Kiesler beschreibt den Prozess später wie folgt: „Die zweisitzige Liegeform hat sich ebenfalls aus dem Prinzip der ununterbrochenen Spannung entwickelt. Ich nahm eine wellenähnliche Form und bog sie, um ein Objekt zu erzeugen, das keinen Anfang und kein Ende hat, und in den konkaven und konvexen Rundungen konnte der Körper dann ruhen. Die Liegeform hatte weder Armlehnen noch Beine und konnte auf beide Seiten gedreht werden. Sie konnte in einen Sessel verwandelt werden, in den Ständer für eine Skulptur oder ein Bild oder auch in einen Tisch oder eine Bank."[68] Zudem geben uns heute die Rekonstruktionspläne, die 2003 im Zuge der Re-Edition dieses Möbels erarbeitet wurden, Aufschluss über den Gestaltungsprozess. Der scheinbar willkürlichen amorphen Form des *Correalistischen Instruments* liegt ein streng geometrisches Konstruktionsschema zu Grunde. In ein Trapez eingeschriebene Kreise definieren die geschwungene Umrisslinie des Korpus. (Abb. S. 119) Grundlage für den *Correalistischen Rocker* bildet hingegen ein Quadrat, welches die geometrische Struktur für die Kreise und die Rundungen vorgibt.[69] (Abb. S. 118, 119) Die Transformation des Sitzmöbels in eine abstrakt-natürliche Grundform schafft die Voraussetzung für dessen weitere Funktionen. Insgesamt erkennt Kiesler 18 verschiedene Verwendungsmöglichkeiten. Im Zusammenhang mit der Theorie von kontinuierlicher Spannung im Raum erfüllt das Möbel eine weit reichende Funktion und ist integraler Bestandteil der Architektur.

Aufgrund des großen Erfolgs, den ihm die Umsetzung von *Art of This Century* einbrachte, wird Kiesler 1947 – nach der Schließung der Galerie – mit der Gestaltung weiterer Ausstellungen beauftragt. Auch in „Bloodflames 1947" in der Hugo Gallery in New York setzt Kiesler das *Correalistische Möbel* ein. (Abb. 75) Im Mai 1947 reist er für den Auftrag, die *Salle des Superstitions* für die „Exposition Internationale du Surréalisme" in der Galerie Maeght zu gestalten, nach Paris. Neben ersten Entwürfen für ein *Endless House* und dem *Manifeste du Corréalisme* entstehen zahlreiche Entwürfe und Studien zu Sitzmöbeln. Ein Briefwechsel von Kiesler mit Wallace K. Harrison liefert eine Begründung für die intensive Beschäftigung mit Design. Harrison ist zu jener Zeit mit ersten Vorverhandlungen für die Errichtung des neuen UNO Hauptquartiers in Manhattan beschäftigt. Als Schüler von Harvey Wiley Corbett arbeitet er in den 30er Jahren an verschiedenen Wohn- und Hochhausprojekten in New York, wie dem Rockefeller Center von 1934 und der Gestaltung des Apartments für Nelson Rockefeller 1937.[70] Harrison, den Kiesler bereits von seiner früheren Tätigkeit als Lektor an der Columbia University kennt, beauftragt ihn 1944 mit der Erstellung eines Ausstellungsdesigns für das „National Council of American-Soviet Friendship" über Amerikanische Architektur in Moskau.[71] Kieslers Layout wird jedoch nicht umgesetzt. Kiesler bietet sich an, die Inneneinrichtung des UNO Hauptquartiers zu gestalten, wird aber nicht mit dem Auftrag betraut.[72]

68 Kiesler 1949 (wie Anm. 3).
69 Dieser Möbelaufbau konnte durch die genauen Studien und Rekonstruktionen von Rene Haentschke und der Firma Wittmann Möbelwerkstätten ermittelt werden.
70 Stern, 1994 (wie Anm. 14) S. 646 ff.
71 Wallace K. Harrison an Friedrich Kiesler am 10.Oktober 1944 und 23. April 1945, Archiv der Kiesler Stiftung Wien und Bogner 1988 (wie Anm. 31), S. 53.
72 Brief von Kiesler an Wallace K. Harrison,12. Januar 1947, Archiv der Kiesler Stiftung Wien.

75 Blick in die Ausstellung „Bloodflames 1947"
    mit *Correalistischem Rocker*, Hugo Gallery,
    New York 1947.
    Installation view of the exhibition "Bloodflames
    1947" with a *Correalistic Rocker*, Hugo Gallery,
    New York, 1947.

76 *Endless House*, Innenraumstudie,
    publiziert in: *Interiors*, 1950.
    Endless House study for interior design,
    published in: *Interiors*, 1950.

77 Kiesler während der Arbeit am Modell für ein
    Endless House, New York ca. 1959.
    Kiesler while shaping a model for
    Endless House, c. 1959.

78 Blick in die *World House Gallery*, New York 1957.
    View of the *World House Gallery*,
    New York 1957.

and in the concave and convex curves, the body could rest. The rest-form had no arms or legs and could be placed either of its sides. It could be transformed into a chair, into a support for sculpture or painting, or into a table or bench."[68] The reconstruction plans elaborated in 2003 in the course of the re-edition of this piece of furniture also explain the design process. The seemingly arbitrary amorphous form of the *Correalist Instrument* was founded on a strictly geometric design pattern. Circles inscribed in a trapezium defined the curving contour of the body. (Fig. p. 119) The basis of the *Correalist Rocker*, in contrast, was a square defining the geometric structure for the circles and curves. (Fig. pp. 118, 119) This lent organic form to the furniture.[69] The transformation of the seat furniture into an abstract, natural basic form provided the conditions for its additional functions. Altogether, Kiesler recognized eighteen different possible uses. In connection with the theory of continuous tension in space, the piece of furniture fulfilled a far-reaching function and was an integral part of the architecture.

Thanks to the great success brought to him by *Art of This Century*, Kiesler was commissioned to design further exhibitions in 1947, after the gallery closed. Kiesler also used the *Correalist Instrument* at the "Bloodflames 1947" exhibition at the Hugo Gallery in New York. (Fig. 75) In May 1947, he traveled to Paris in connection with his contract to design the *Salle des Superstitions* for the "Exposition Internationale du Surréalisme" at the Maeght Gallery. In addition to the first drafts for an *Endless House* and the *Manifeste du Corréalisme*, he also did numerous plans and studies for seat furniture. Correspondence between Kiesler and Wallace K. Harrison provides grounds for his in-depth occupation with design. At this time, Harrison was involved in preliminary negotiations for construction of the new UN headquarters in Manhattan. As a student of Harvey Wiley Corbett, he had worked on various housing and tower-block projects in New York in the thirties, for example the Rockefeller Center in 1934 and designs for Nelson Rockefeller's apartment in 1937.[70] Harrison, whom Kiesler had already known from his early work as a junior university teacher at Columbia University, commissioned him on behalf of the "National Council of American-Soviet Friendship Inc." in 1944 to create a layout for an exhibition of American architecture in Moscow.[71] However, Kiesler's exhibition design was not carried out. Kiesler offered to design the interior of the UN headquarters, but did not receive the contract.[72]

After that, Kiesler flew to Paris on May 21 in order to set up the "Exposition Internationale du Surréalisme" conceived by André Breton and Marcel Duchamp. This project gave him another opportunity to lend form to his correalistic conception of space. On his return, Kiesler began to focus completely on architecture and art. Kiesler's exploration of furniture design ended with a number of studies on lounger furniture. In these studies, he reduced the structure of the

68 Kiesler 1949 (cf. note 3).
69 This furniture structure was ascertained by detailed studies and reconstructions performed by Rene Haentschke
    and Wittmann Möbelwerkstätten.
70 Stern, 1994 (cf. note 14) p. 646 ff.
71 Wallace K. Harrison to Frederick Kiesler on October 10, 1944, and April 23, 1945, Archive of the Kiesler Foundation
    Vienna and Bogner 1988 (cf. note 31), p. 53.
72 Letter from Kiesler to Wallace K. Harrison, January 12, 1947, Archive of the Kiesler Foundation Vienna.

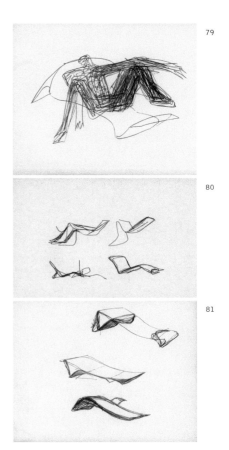

Danach fliegt Kiesler am 27. Mai nach Paris, um die von André Breton und Marcel Duchamp konzipierte „Exposition Internationale du Surréalisme" aufzu-bauen. Dieses Projekt bietet ihm eine weitere Möglichkeit, seiner correalistischen Raumauffassung Gestalt zu verleihen. Nach seiner Rückkehr wendet sich Kiesler ganz der Architektur und der Kunst zu. Mit einigen Studien zu Liegemöbeln endet Kieslers Auseinandersetzung mit Möbeldesign. Er reduziert hier die Struktur des Möbels auf die reine Form der Liegefläche. Das Möbel konstituiert sich wie ein frei im Raum schwebendes Objekt, seine Gestalt ist Ausdruck der wechsel-seitigen Kräfte: „Wenn wir einen Sessel benutzen, nehmen wir seine Energie in uns auf."[73] (Abb. 79-81)

Das Konzept des *Endless House* als Einfamilienhaus beschäftigt Kiesler bis in die frühen 60er Jahre. Darin entwickelt er seine Idee eines flexiblen, kontinuier-lichen Raumes weiter. (Abb. 76-77) Wie das *Correalistische Instrument* ein Werkzeug zur Verbindung von Architektur, Möbel und dem Menschen ist, so ist das *Endless House* die Einheit von komplexen Relationen zwischen dem Raum und seinen Bewohnern. Einer Überlieferung zufolge, propagiert Kiesler sein *Endless House* in den 60er Jahren als Museumsbau in Cleveland, Ohio. Damit hätte er den Anspruch auf eine „Architektur der Zusammenhänge" im Sinne des Gesamtkunst-werk-Gedankens ein weiteres Mal eingelöst. Mit der Erweiterung des Einfamilien-hauses zur Museumsarchitektur würde sich auch Theo van Doesburgs Vision bewahrheiten: Die Zusammenführung des abstrakten Kunstraums mit der flexiblen Gestaltung sozialer Realitäten. Die Regeln für diese Verbindung sind für Kiesler in den gesellschaftlichen Bedürfnissen angelegt. „Das *Endless House* ist keine amor-phe, für alles offene Form. Im Gegenteil, seine Struktur weist strikte Grenzen auf, die dem Ausmaß unserer Bedürfnisse entsprechen. Seine Gestalt und Form werden von inhärenten Lebenskräften bestimmt, und nicht von Bauvorschriften oder Aus-stattungslaunen und -moden."[74] Eine Haltung, der Kiesler in seiner Arbeit stets treu geblieben ist.

73   Frederick Kiesler, Typoskript, ca. 1938-1941, Archiv der Kiesler Stiftung Wien.
74   Frederick Kiesler, *Inside the Endless House*, New York 1966, S. 566. (Orig. Zit. in Engl.)

79-81   Entwürfe zu einer Liege, ca. 1950.

Sketches for a lounge chair, c. 1950.

furniture to the pure form of the reclining surface. The piece of furniture is constituted like an object hovering freely in space, its form is the expression of interacting forces: "When we use a chair we absorb its energy."[73] (Fig. 79-81)

Kiesler continued to work on the concept of the *Endless House* as a family dwelling until the early sixties. In this concept he further developed his idea of a flexible, continuous space. (Fig. 76-77) Just as the *Correalist Instrument* is a tool for combining architecture, furniture and the human being, so too is the *Endless House* the unification of complex relations of space and its inhabitants. According to one source, Kiesler promoted his *Endless House* in the sixties as a museum building, wanting to see it built in Cleveland, Ohio. As such, he would once again have fulfilled the requirement of an "architecture of correlations" in the sense of the idea of a total art work. Enlarging the house into museum architecture would also confirm Theo van Doesburg's vision: to unite the abstract space of art with the flexible design of social realities. Kiesler saw the rules governing this link entrenched in social needs. In order to rule out any misunderstandings, he observed in 1965, shortly before his death, "The Endless House is not amorphous, not a free-for-all form. On the contrary its construction has strict boundaries according to the scale of our living. Its shape and form are determined by inherent life forces, not by building code standards or the vagaries of décor fads."[74] A stance to which Kiesler always remained true in his work.

73   Frederick Kiesler, typescript, c. 1938-1941, Archive of the Kiesler Foundation Vienna.
74   Frederick Kiesler, *Inside the Endless House*, New York 1966, p. 566.

Correalistische Möbel
Correalist Furniture

83

84-86   Studien zum *Correalistischen Rocker*, 1942.

          Studies for *Correalist Rocker*, 1942.

87   Kiesler auf einem *Correalistischen Rocker*
          in der Surrealistischen Galerie, *Art of
          This Century*, New York 1942.
          Foto: Berenice Abbott.

          Kiesler sitting on a *Correalist Rocker*
          in the Surrealist Gallery, *Art of This
          Century*, New York 1942.

          Photograph by Berenice Abbott.

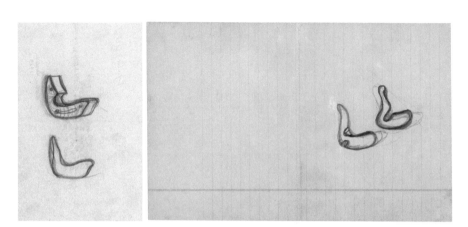

84   85

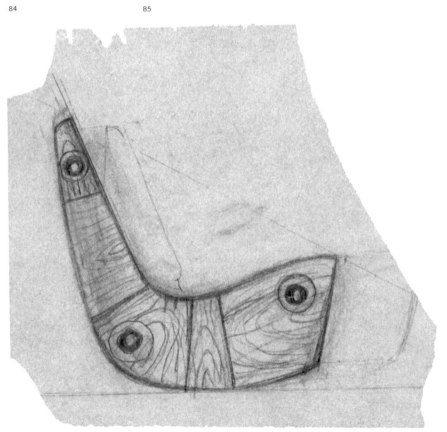

86

88-89   Studie zum *Correalistischen Instrument*, 1942.

Study for *Correalist Instrument*, 1942.

90   *Correalistische Instrumente* als Sockel für

Skulpturen in der Abstrakten Galerie,

Art of This Century, New York 1942.

Foto: Berenice Abbott.

Correalist Instruments used as supports

for sculptures in the Abstract Gallery,

Art of This Century, New York 1942.

Photograph by Berenice Abbott.

88

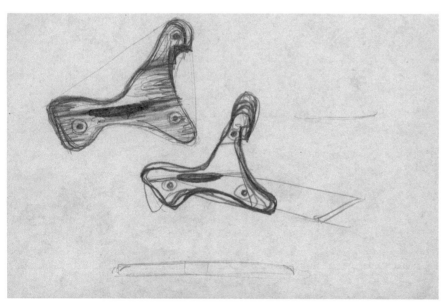

89

90

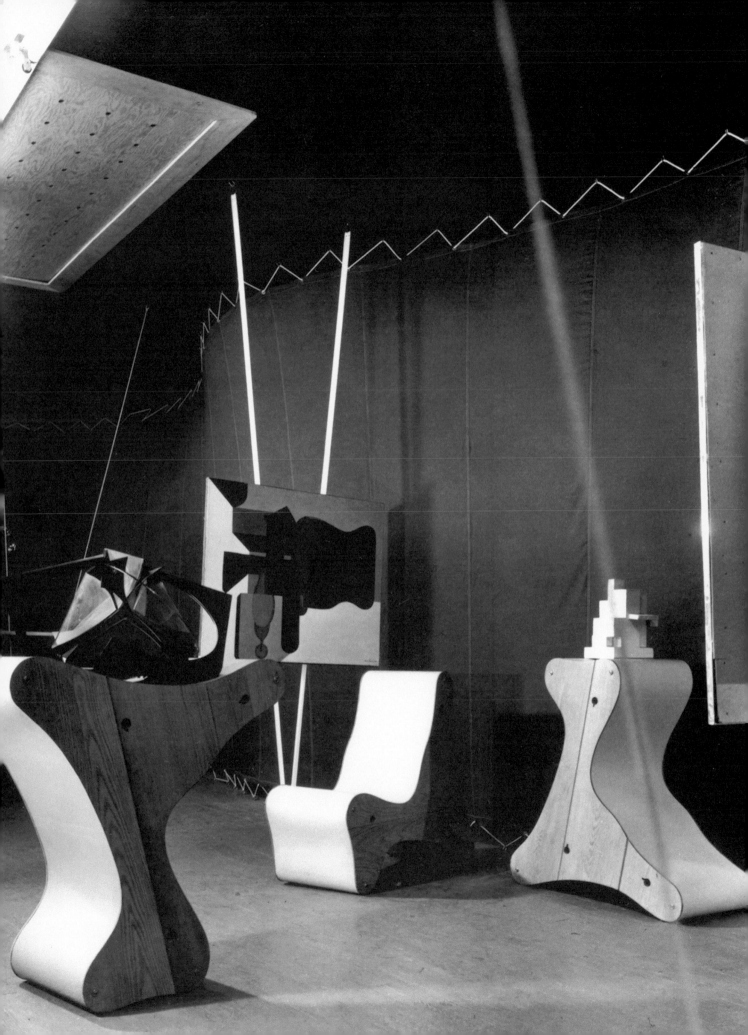

91 Zeichnung zu drei Funktionen des *Correalistischen*
    Instruments, 1942-43.
    Drawing of three functions of a *Correalist*
    Instrument, 1942-43.

92 Studie zu vier Funktionen des *Correalistischen*
    Instruments, publiziert in: *VVV*, März 1943.
    Study of four functions of a *Correalist*
    Instrument, published in: *VVV*, March 1943.

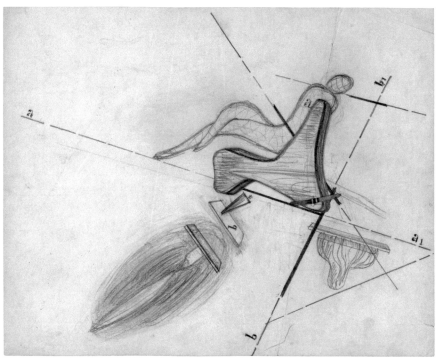

91

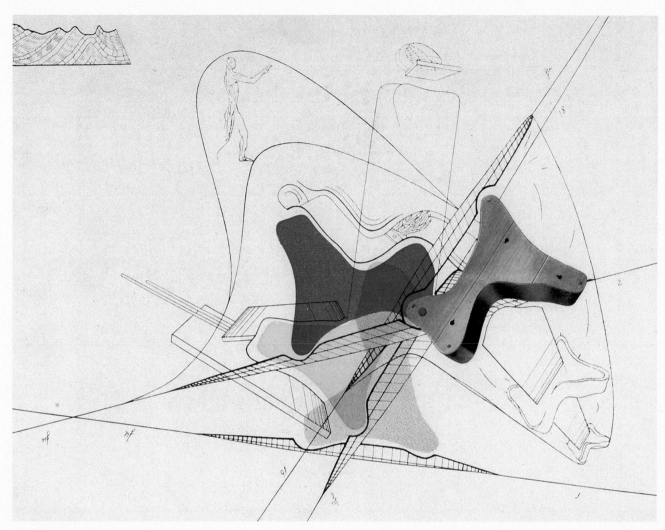

92

93 Schaubild zu achtzehn Funktionen des
    Correalistischen Instruments, publiziert in:
    Architectural Forum, Februar 1943.
    Chart of eighteen functions of a *Correalist
    Instrument,* published in: *Architectural Forum,*
    February 1943.

94 *Correalistische Möbel* für *Art of This Century,*
    New York, 1942, Sammlung Ron Warren
    und Joshua Mack, New York.
    Foto: Zindman/Fremont.
    Correalist Furniture for *Art of This Century,*
    New York, 1942, Collection Ron Warren
    and Joshua Mack, New York.
    Photograph by Zindman/Fremont.

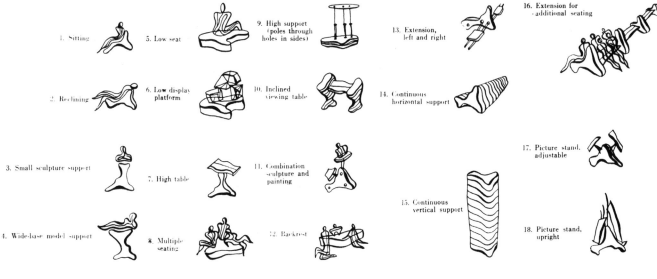

94

95 Variante eines *Correalistischen Instruments*,
    Museum of Modern Art, New York 1942.
    Variation of a *Correalist Instrument,* Museum
    of Modern Art, New York 1942.

96 Studie zu einer Variante des *Correalistischen
    Instruments*, 1942.
    Study for a variation of *Correalist Instrument,* 1942.

97 Studie zu den Funktionen der *Correalistischen
    Möbel*, 1942.
    Study for the different functions of the
    Correalist Furniture, 1942.

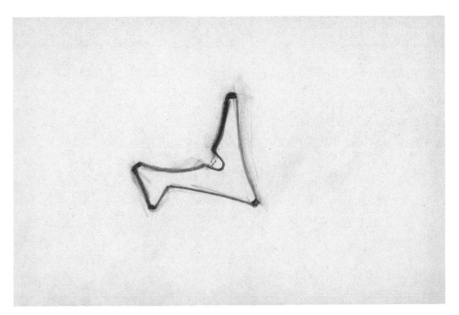

96

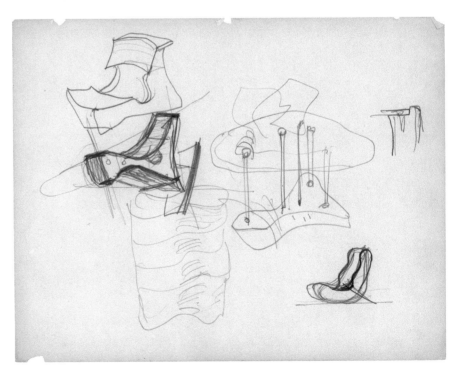

97

88

Möbelentwürfe 1947
Furniture Designs 1947

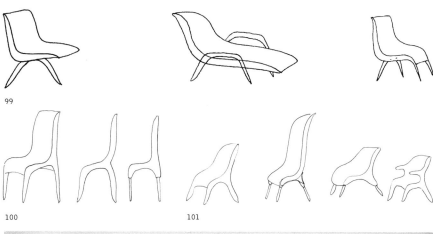

99

100   101

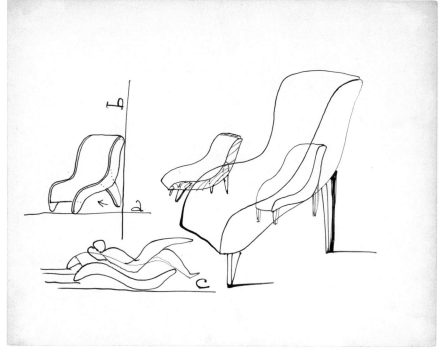

Party-Beach

103

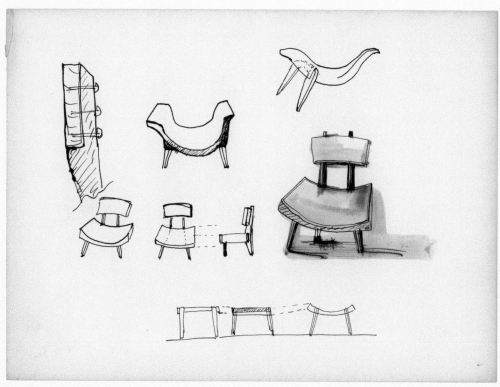

104

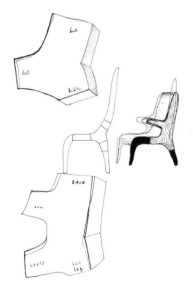

105

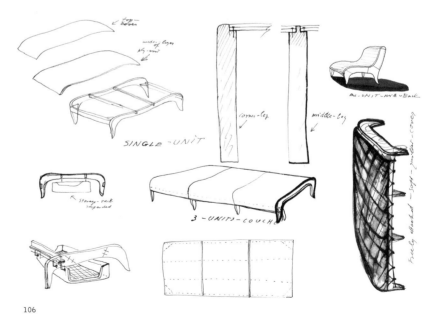

106

107 Studie zu einer Variante des
Correalistischen Instruments, ca. 1947,
Sammlung Barbara Pine, New York.
Study for a variation of the
Correalist Instrument, c. 1947,
Collection Barbara Pine, New York.

108 Studien zu Stuhl und Bank, Paris 1947.
Studies for chair and bench, Paris 1947.

109 Studie zu einer Variante des *Correalistischen
Instruments*, ca. 1947.
Study for a variation of the *Correalist
Instrument*, c. 1947.

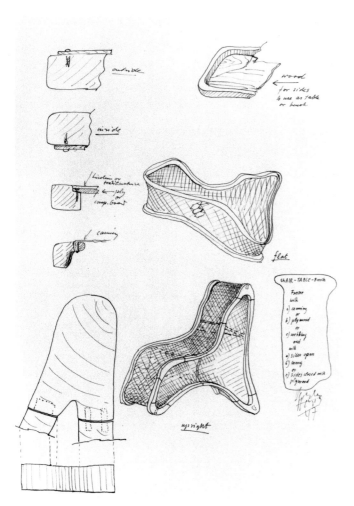

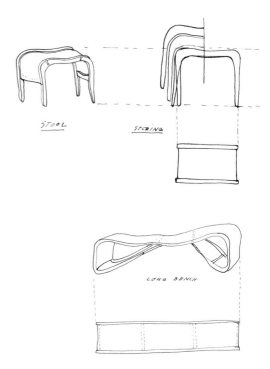

107

108

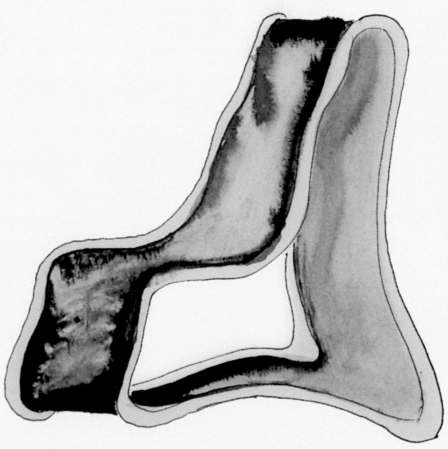

109

110 Friedrich Kiesler in seinem Apartment mit einem Sessel
von Alvar Aalto, New York ca. 1950. Foto: Ben Schnall.
Frederick Kiesler in his apartment with a chair by
Alvar Aalto, c. 1950. Photograph by Ben Schnall.

Zur Re-Edition Friedrich Kiesler:
On the Re-edition Frederick Kiesler:
Nucleus of Forces

Tulga Beyerle

Zur Re-Edition Friedrich Kiesler:
Nucleus of Forces

Kein Klassiker

Stellt sich die Herausforderung, historische Möbel wieder aufzulegen, wird die Frage aufgeworfen, warum diese und keine anderen, warum Friedrich Kiesler und nicht Josef Frank, um nur ein Beispiel zu nennen. Eine Antwort findet sich bereits in dem Begriff „historisch", welcher der Faszination von Kieslers Arbeiten nicht nur nicht gerecht wird, sondern in keiner Weise angemessen scheint.

Wenn die besten Stücke Mies van der Rohes heutzutage als „Klassiker" Teil unserer modernen Wohnkultur geworden sind, so ist Kieslers Möbelentwürfen diese Ehre in diesem Ausmaß noch nicht widerfahren. Natürlich zeichnet einen „Klassiker" die Ausgewogenheit der Proportionen aus, ebenso eine gewisse „Zeitlosigkeit" des Entwurfs, der Generationen überdauert und heute noch „Modernität" in Anspruch nimmt. Und natürlich sind wir der Überzeugung, dass auch die Entwürfe Friedrich Kieslers ihren Platz in der Designgeschichte einnehmen. Aber vielmehr noch sind wir der Überzeugung, dass sie, wegen der ihnen zu Grunde liegenden Philosophie, im Besonderen für das zeitgenössische, aktuelle Designgeschehen Bedeutung haben. So bedarf es vor allem einer tief greifenden Auseinandersetzung mit der Kieslerschen Entwurfsphilosophie, um die Aktualität der hier neu aufgelegten Möbel, alle im Zeitraum der frühen 30er und 40er Jahre des letzten Jahrhunderts entworfen, zu verstehen.

Friedrich Kiesler war immer ein ausgesprochener Kritiker der Moderne. Viele seiner Texte bezogen sich explizit auf die Konzepte und Entwürfe von Le Corbusier und Mies van der Rohe, denen er für das Abwerfen alter Lasten aus historistischen Epochen, für die notwendige Zäsur und damit verbundene Öffnung für ein modernes Bauen Respekt zollte. „Der abstrakte Funktionalismus war eine freiwillige Diät nach den ausschweifenden Jahren der viktorianischen Epoche. Da Diät den verfetteten Architekturkörper wieder in Ordnung gebracht hat, ist nicht mehr genügend Ursache vorhanden, diese Diät fortzusetzen. Die freiwillige Beschränkung auf Hygiene, ästhetische und physische, hat ihre Schuldigkeit mit Erfolg getan."[1] Kieslers Auseinandersetzung mit Design, mit Architektur führte ihn zu einer ganzheitlichen Analyse der notwendigen Entwurfsaufgaben, deren zentraler Mittelpunkt immer der Mensch war, (Abb. 111, 112) in all seiner Komplexität und auch in all seiner Unzulänglichkeit. Nicht nur die Möglichkeiten neuer Technologien oder die Suche nach der reinen, klaren Form bewegten Kiesler, sondern vor allem die Suche nach dem Ursprung jener Kräfte, die auf jede Entwicklung wirken würden. „Was immer für eine Kreatur daraus entsteht, sie ist niemals flach im Gefühl, sondern dreidimensional. Wie ein Ball sucht sie nach Koordination. Sie atmet mit allen Sinnen Kontakt. Sie hängt gleicherweise mit Sichtbarem, Tastbarem, Riechbarem und Unsichtbarem und nicht-unmittelbar-Tastbarem, nicht-automatisch-Riechbarem

1   Frederick Kiesler, *Manifest des Correalismus*, Typoskript, 1947, Archiv der Kiesler Stiftung Wien.

On the Re-edition Frederick Kiesler: Nucleus of Forces

Not a classic

Faced with the challenge of creating a re-edition of historical furniture, the question arises as to why this and not some other furniture, why Frederick Kiesler and not Josef Frank, just to give an example. One answer is already found in the term "historical", that not only fails to do justice to the fascination of Kiesler's works, but which also appears completely inappropriate.

If, today, the best of Mies van der Rohe's pieces have become a "classic" part of our modern domestic culture, Kiesler's furniture designs have yet to receive this level of honour. Naturally, a "classic" stands out due to the harmony of its proportions, along with a certain "timelessness" of the design, that lives on for generations and that remains "modern" even today. And, naturally, we are convinced that Frederick Kiesler's designs have equally found their place in the history of design. But, more to the point, we are convinced that, by merit of their underlying philosophy, they are relevant above all in terms of contemporary, current design. Consequently, we above all need to explore Kiesler's design philosophy in great depth so as to comprehend the contemporary relevance of the furniture now to be reproduced, all of which was designed in the period of the early nineteen-thirties and forties.

Frederick Kiesler was always a trenchant critic of modernism. Many of his writings made explicit reference to the designs of Le Corbusier and Mies van der Rohe, whom he respected for casting off the old burdens from historical eras, for the necessary break with the past, and for consequently opening the way for modern building. "Abstract Functionalism was a voluntary diet following the dissolute years of the Victorian era. Now that the diet has put the fatty body of architecture back into shape, there is no reason to continue this diet. The voluntary restriction to hygiene, both aesthetic and physical, has successfully served its purpose."[1] Kiesler's investigation of design and architecture led him to a holistic analysis of the necessary design tasks, whose central focus has ever been the human being, (Fig. 111, 112) with all his complexity and all his shortcomings. Not only the possibilities of new technologies or the search for pure, clear form motivated Kiesler, but above all the search for the origin of the forces that acted on every development. "Whatever creature results, it never has the feel of being flat, but is rather three-dimensional. Like a ball it searches for coordination. It breathes contact with all its senses. It is connected by an infinite number of bonds, beams, waves and molecular bridges with what is visible, tangible, smellable and invisible and not immediately tangible, not automatically smellable, and itself casts out a myriad of threads so as to entwine itself even more into life. It (the creature) cannot exist without others.

1   Frederick Kiesler, *Manifest des Correalismus*, typescript, 1947, Archive of the Kiesler Foundation Vienna. (Orig. quot. in Ger.)

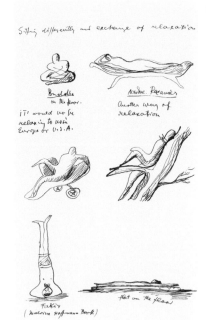

durch unendlich viele Bande, Strahlen, Wellen und Molekularbrücken zusammen, und wirft selber eine Myriade von Fäden aus, um sich noch mehr ins Leben zu verstricken. Sie (die Kreatur) kann ohne Andere nicht leben. Ihr Leben ist ein Mit-Leben. Ihre Realität ist eine Co-Realität. Ihr Realismus der Verwirklichung ist ein Co-Realismus."[2] Der Grundriss, die Form, die jeweils aktuelle Mode interessierten Friedrich Kiesler nicht so sehr wie die Erforschung grundsätzlicher Fragen des Lebens, um dem modernen Menschen eine zeitgemäße Lebensqualität bieten zu können. Ein Objekt von Friedrich Kiesler entworfen ist nicht als Solitär zu sehen, sondern immer im Zusammenhang mit Raum, Bewegung, mit dem Menschen. Daher entsteht die Multifunktionalität der Stücke aus der Erkenntnis, dass eine einmalig zugeordnete Funktion der Dynamik und Flexibilität unserem modernen Leben nicht gerecht werden kann, dass das Objekt selbst dynamische Bewegung zulassen müsse und sich selbst in einem Prozess der Veränderung befinde. Friedrich Kieslers künstlerisches Interesse war von dem Wunsch geprägt, die Veränderung unserer Wahrnehmung sowie eine flexible Objektnutzung zu unserer Bedürfnisbefriedigung zu erreichen. Es ist daher nicht verwunderlich, wenn er in dem Patentansuchen zur *Party Lounge* schreibt: „Es ist ersichtlich, dass in Bezug auf das Design und die Konstruktionsdetails meiner verbesserten Lounge viele Änderungen möglich sind, ohne dass dies etwas am Charakter der vorliegenden Erfindung ändern würde. Und obwohl ich spezifische Konstruktionsformen meiner Erfindung gezeigt und beschrieben habe, möchte ich dies nicht als Beschränkung meiner selbst auf die hierin gezeigte und beschriebene Konstruktion verstanden wissen. Im Besonderen möchte ich festhalten, dass ich die Verwendung besagter Erfindung im Zusammenhang mit vielen anderen Geräten und Möbelstücken in Erwägung ziehe, wie zum Beispiel mit Stühlen, Sesseln, Fauteuils, Ruhebetten, Sofas, Tischen und ähnlichem."[3]

Kieslers Konzepte waren im Gegensatz zu den Entwürfen seiner Zeitgenossen nicht so sehr einem bestimmten Stil oder dem Anspruch der Moderne verpflichtet, sondern trugen Veränderung, Weiterentwicklung und Offenheit für Neues in sich. Vielleicht scheint deshalb der Begriff „Klassiker" für Kieslers Werk nicht zutreffend, da dieses bis heute so unzulänglich und gleichzeitig so spannend wie der Mensch selbst ist, ein „Nucleus of Forces" für neue Funktionen, neue Ideen und neue Objektkreationen.

Kiesler inspiriert

Friedrich Kiesler konnte nur wenige seiner Ideen in die Praxis umsetzen, und hat dennoch sowohl durch seine Publikationen wie auch durch die wenigen realisierten Möbel- und Architekturentwürfe Generationen von Designern und Architekten beeinflusst. Es bedarf sicher eines eigenen Forschungsprojektes, die genauen Einflüsse Kieslers auf die nach ihm kommenden Designgenerationen zu untersuchen, aber schon bei oberflächlicher Betrachtung zeitgenössischer Entwürfe fallen einem zahlreiche Ähnlichkeiten und Parallelen ins Auge. Wichtig ist dabei, die Übernahme rein formaler Aspekte vom theoretischen Einfluss auf zeitgenössisches

2   Ebd.
3   Patent zur *Party Lounge* vom 22. August 1939, Archiv der Kiesler Stiftung Wien. (Orig. Zit. in Engl.)

Its existence is a co-existence. Its reality a co-reality. Its realism of realization is a Co-Realism."[2] The ground plan, the form, the current fashion did not interest Frederick Kiesler as much as investigating fundamental questions of life, with the aim of offering modern-day people a modern quality of life. An object designed by Frederick Kiesler should not be regarded as a solitary item, but rather always in connection with space, motion, and the human being. Hence, the multifunctionality of the objects results from the realization that a function of dynamics and flexibility that is assigned only once cannot do justice to our modern life, that the object itself would have to permit dynamic motion and itself be in a process of change. Frederick Kiesler's interest as an artist was founded on the desire to achieve a change in our perception and a flexible use of objects in order to satisfy our needs. It is therefore no surprise when he writes in a patent application for the *Party Lounge*, "It will be obvious that many changes may be made in the design and the structural details of my improved lounge without departing from the spirit of the present invention. And although I have shown and described specific forms of construction of my invention, I do not wish to be understood as limiting myself to the exact construction shown and described herein. It should be noted particularly that I contemplate the use of my said invention in connection with many other devices and pieces of furniture, such as for inst.: chairs, easy-chairs, fauteuils, daybeds, sofas, tables and the like."[3]

Unlike the designs of his contemporaries, Kiesler's concepts were not so much committed to a particular style or claim to modernism, but rather already inherently embraced change, further development, and openness for novelties. Perhaps this is why the term "classic" does not seem appropriate when describing Kiesler's work, which has, to this day, remained as deficient and at the same time as exciting as the human being himself, a "Nucleus of Forces" for new functions, new ideas, and new object creations.

99

Kiesler inspires

Frederick Kiesler was only able to put a few of his ideas into practice, and nevertheless influenced generations of designers and architects both with his publications and with the few furniture and architecture designs that were actually built. It would certainly take a dedicated research project to investigate the exact influence of Kiesler on later design generations, but numerous similarities and parallels become obvious even on superficial examination of contemporary designs. The important thing is to distinguish between the adoption of purely formal aspects and his theoretical influence on contemporary design. For in their expressive form and function, Kiesler's furniture designs were evidently often a source of inspiration for designers and architects alike. References to Kiesler's works are found, above all, in the work of Ron Arad, but equally so in the designs of Marc Newson or Nigel Coates, just as the much published sofa by Francesco Binfarè, *flap* or *damier* for Edra seems to be an offspring of the *Party*

2   Op. cit.
3   Patent for the *Party Lounge* of August 22, 1939, Archive of the Kiesler Foundation Vienna.

Design zu trennen. Denn offensichtlich waren Kieslers Möbelentwürfe in ihrer expressiven Form und Funktion oft Quelle der Inspiration für Designer wie für Architekten. Ron Arad allen voran, aber auch in den Entwürfen von Marc Newson oder Nigel Coates finden sich Bezüge zu den Arbeiten Kieslers, ebenso wie das viel publizierte Sofa von Francesco Binfarè *flap* oder *damier* für Edra Nachkommen der *Party Lounge* zu sein scheinen. (Abb. 113) Zeitgenössische Architektur integriert interdisziplinäre Forschung in ihre Ansätze und Entwicklungen, aber in welcher Form geschieht dies im zeitgenössischen Design? Die wissenschaftlichen und konzeptuellen Ansätze von Friedrich Kiesler finden sich in den aktuellen Forschungsbestrebungen der modernen Designtheorie wieder. Im Gegensatz zu einer traditionellen eher kunsthistorisch angelegten Betrachtungsweise verfolgt diese einen zeitgemäßen Visual Culture Ansatz, der ethnologische bzw. anthropologische Forschungsmethoden ebenso integriert wie die zeitgenössische soziologische Forschung der Gebrauchs- und Alltagskultur. So finden sich heute in der gegenwärtigen Designtheorie die interdisziplinären und damals revolutionären Ideen Kieslers wieder. Ebenso wie zwischen Designtheorie und -praxis oft kaum Verbindungen und Beziehungen zu existieren scheinen, so kann man nicht behaupten, dass die grundsätzlichen Fragen und daraus entwickelten Theorien Kieslers alleiniger Ausgangspunkt für die offensichtlich von ihm inspirierten Objekte sind. Aber vielleicht spielt die Frage nach dem eigentlichen Ursprung auch keine besondere Rolle, da sich die Ideen, der Nucleus, der uns von Kiesler gegeben wurde, auf Grund der ihm innewohnenden Kraft aus sich selbst heraus und ohne bewusstes Aufgreifen der zu Grunde liegenden Inhalte weiter entwickeln konnte und so auf viele Nachkommen einwirkte.

Man muss zur Kenntnis nehmen, dass trotz der Vielfalt und der Freiheit, in der sich heutiges Design entwickelt, wenig originär Neues und Anderes entsteht. Architektur scheint sich in viel radikalerer Form mit aktuellen gesellschaftlichen Entwicklungen und Forschungen auseinander zu setzen und nach Antworten darauf zu suchen. Die wenigen Designer und Designerinnen, deren Arbeiten mögliche und oft sehr konzeptionelle Antworten auf aktuelle Fragen unsere Zeit anbieten, beziehen sich meist nicht direkt auf Kiesler. Dennoch seien sie in diesem Zusammenhang erwähnt, da DesignerInnen wie Dunne and Raby, Michael Anastassiades, Tord Boontje, Hella Jongerius, Jurgen Bey (Abb. 114) oder Robert Stadler (Abb. 115) ebenso wie Kiesler auf den Menschen eingehen, ihn, den Menschen, zum zentralen Thema ihrer Arbeit machen. Und zwar den Menschen mit all seinen Bedürfnissen, in seinem unbewussten wie bewussten Dasein, den Menschen als ein Phänomen in Bewegung, in ewiger Unvollendetheit.

Wir haben die Chance in der Auseinandersetzung mit Kiesler und über die selbstgestellte Aufgabe der Re-Editionen nicht nur seine formale Sprache, sondern auch seine philosophischen wie konzeptuellen Thesen als Inspirationsquelle zu nutzen.

Lernen von Kiesler

Es sollte nicht unerwähnt bleiben, dass die hier vorgestellten Arbeiten von Friedrich Kiesler ihrer Zeit voraus waren. Was für ihn vielleicht schwierig war,

Lounge. (Fig. 113) Contemporary architecture integrates interdisciplinary research into its approaches and developments, but in what form does this occur in contemporary design? Frederick Kiesler's scientific and conceptual approaches are certainly to be found in current research approaches of modern design theory. Unlike a traditional, rather art historical examination, this investigation takes a modern visual culture approach, integrating ethnological and anthropological research methods as well as contemporary sociological research of utility and everyday culture. Today, then, Kiesler's interdisciplinary, at the time revolutionary approaches are again found in current design theory. Just as there often seem to be hardly any links and relations between design theory and practice, nor can we claim that the fundamental questions investigated by Kiesler and his derived theories are the sole point of departure for the objects he so obviously inspired. But perhaps the question as to the true origin does not play such a crucial role, as the ideas, the nucleus that Kiesler gave us was, thanks to its inherent power, able to evolve on its own momentum and without intentionally focusing on the underlying content, and thus influence many offspring.

It must be noted that, for all the variety and freedom with which modern design is developed, there is little about it that is new or original. Architecture would seem to explore current social developments and research far more radically, searching for answers to the questions involved. The few designers whose work offers possible, often conceptual, answers to current questions, usually do not make immediate reference to Kiesler. And yet mention should be made of them in this context, as – just like Kiesler – such designers as Dunne and Raby, Michael Anastassiades, Tord Boontje, Hella Jongerius, Jurgen Bey (Fig. 114) or Robert Stadler (Fig. 115) equally show an interest in the human being, making him the very focus of their work. That is to say, the human being with all his needs, in his unconscious and conscious existence, the human being as a phenomenon in motion, in eternal incompletion.

101

In our examination of Kiesler and in the re-edition task we have set ourselves, we have the opportunity to take advantage not only of his formal language, but also his philosophical and conceptual theories as a source of inspiration.

Learning from Kiesler

It should not be left unmentioned that the works of Frederick Kiesler presented here were ahead of their time. What may have been difficult for him, is a stroke of luck for us, for today we now have the pleasure of enjoying this exciting furniture, for example the *Party Lounge*, the *Bed Couch*, the *Correalistic Furniture*, and the *Correalist Rocker*. The quality of these pieces, their ergonomy, speaks for itself and seamlessly takes its place in the sophisticated Wittmann design collection.

But what can we learn from Kiesler today? An important fact would seem to be that, in developing the furniture, Frederick Kiesler did not proceed on the

ist für uns ein Glück, da wir das Vergnügen haben, uns jetzt und heute an den spannenden Möbeln, wie der *Party Lounge*, der *Bed Couch*, dem *Correalistischen Instrument* und dem *Correalistischen Rocker* zu erfreuen. Die Qualität dieser Stücke, ihre Bedarfsorientiertheit spricht für sich und reiht sich nahtlos in die anspruchsvolle Designkollektion von Wittmann ein.

Aber was können wir von Kiesler heute lernen? Wesentlich scheint uns die Tatsache, dass Friedrich Kiesler in der Entwicklung der Möbel nicht von einem Sofa, dem Bett, der Badewanne oder dem Bücherregal als Objekt ausging, sondern von der Funktion des Sitzens, Schlafens, des Badens oder der Bücheraufbewahrung. Diese grundsätzliche Herangehensweise bezeichnet einen spannenden Aspekt in Kieslers Schaffen. Eine weitere zentrale Rolle in seinen Überlegungen nimmt, wie schon erwähnt, der Mensch ein, der in all seinen Texten und auch Arbeiten Erwähnung findet. Wenn man also die Absicht verfolgt, die Ideen Kieslers ins Heute zu transferieren, dann muss man sich mit unserem heutigen Dasein beschäftigen, man muss Kieslers Idee des Nucleus verfolgen und diesen in Beziehung setzen zu den herrschenden Kräften, den Energien, die aus den verschiedenen Feldern auf uns, auf unsere Ideen, auf die von uns geschaffenen Objekte wirken. Hier zeigt sich ein moderner Ansatz nicht nur der Interdisziplinarität, sondern auch des Netzwerkgedankens, wie er sich derzeit durch viele Sparten unserer Forschung zieht – nur nicht unbedingt durch das populäre zeitgenössische Design. In diesem Sinne sei es mir auch erlaubt, kritische Worte Friedrich Kieslers in Erinnerung zu rufen: „Das Ziel (einer derartigen Beseitigung der ewigen Krise in der Architektur) kann nur in der Einführung eines wissenschaftlichen Maßstabes für den Umgang mit Designproblemen bestehen, eines Maßstabes, der nicht aus dem Studium der architektonischen Vergangenheit oder Gegenwart erwachsen, sondern sich ausschließlich durch die Beobachtung von Lebensprozessen ergeben kann."[4] Wobei ich die Aufmerksamkeit zum einen auf das Studieren von Lebensprozessen lenken möchte (wie es unter anderem von manchen der oben erwähnten DesignerInnen durchaus verfolgt wird), zum anderen auf eine notwendige Vernetzung mit anderen Disziplinen. Denn folgt man Kiesler, dann bedeutet Correalismus ein gleichzeitiges Existieren vieler Kräfte und verlangt eine entsprechende Offenheit des Sehens, des Beobachtens, des Schweigens und des Lernens. Vielleicht können wir auch noch etwas von Kiesler übernehmen – die Fähigkeit, auch Unerklärliches als eine weitere Co-Realität in unser Leben zu integrieren.

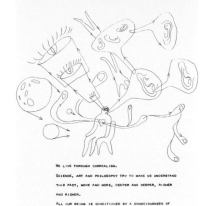

„Wir leben durch den Correalismus. Wissenschaft, Kunst und Philosophie versuchen, uns diese Tatsache immer stärker und auf immer tieferen und umfassenderen Ebenen begreiflich zu machen. Unser ganzes Sein ist durch das Bewusstsein des Correalismus bestimmt." (Abb. 118)

4   Frederick Kiesler, *The Laboratory for Design Correlation*, Typoskript, 1937–41, Archiv der Kiesler Stiftung Wien.

116 Im Rahmen der Ausstellung *Friedrich Kiesler:*
     Art of This Century 1942 im MMK Frankfurt,
     2002-03, wurden die *Correalistischen Möbel*
     zusammen mit der Serie TODAY von
     On Kawara gezeigt.
     Foto: Axel Schneider.
     In the context of the show *Friedrich Kiesler:*
     Art of This Century 1942 in the MMK Frankfurt,
     2002-03, the *Correalist Furniture* was displayed
     together with the serie TODAY of On Kawara.
     Photograph by Axel Schneider.

117 Während der Ausstellung *Peggy and Kiesler.*
     The Collector and the Visionary in Venedig,
     2003-05, waren die *Correalistischen*
     Möbel integrativer Bestandteil der
     Peggy Guggenheim Collection.
     Foto: Sergio Martucci.
     During the exhibition Peggy and Kiesler.
     The Collector and the Visionary in Venice,
     2003-05, the *Correalist Furniture* was integrated
     into the Peggy Guggenheim Collection.
     Photograph by Sergio Martucci.

118 Illustration zur Theorie des *Correalismus,*
     New York 1937-41.
     Illustration for the Theory of *Correalism,*
     New York 1937-41.

basis of a sofa, bed, bathtub or bookshelf as an object, but rather on the basis of the function of sitting, sleeping, bathing or storing books. This fundamental approach is an exciting aspect in Kiesler's work. As mentioned above, the human being assumes another crucial role in his considerations and is mentioned in all his writings and indeed works. If, then, we pursue the intention of transferring Kiesler's ideas into the modern world, we must consider our modern existence, following Kiesler's idea of the nucleus and relating this to the dominant forces, the energies acting on us from the various fields, on our ideas, and on the objects we create. Here we see a modern approach not only of interdisciplinarity but also of networking, as currently pervades many fields of our research – albeit not necessarily popular contemporary design. On this note allow me to recall Frederick Kiesler's critical words: "The goal (of such an elimination of the perennial crisis in architecture) can only be found in establishing a scientific scale for the approach to design problems; a scale which cannot grow out of studies of architectural past or present, but which can only be found in the light of studying life processes".[4] On the one hand, I would like to draw attention to studying life processes (as, among others, some of the aforementioned designers indeed do), and to the necessity of networking with other disciplines on the other. For according to Kiesler, correalism implies the simultaneous existence of many forces and demands an associated openness of seeing, observing, remaining silent, and learning. Perhaps we can adopt something else from Kiesler, too – the ability to integrate the inexplicable into our life as another co-reality.

"We live through Correalism. Science, Art and Philosophy try to make us understand this fact, more and more, deeper and deeper, richer and richer. All our being is conditioned by a consciousness of Correalism." (Fig. 118)

4   Frederick Kiesler, *The Laboratory for Design Correlation,* Typoskript, 1937-41, Archive of the Kiesler Foundation Vienna.
    (Orig. quot. in Ger.)

„Insofern als meine Lounge Platz für eine ganze Party auf
einmal bietet, nenne ich meine Lounge *Party Lounge*." (Friedrich Kiesler, 1939)

"Inasmuch as my new lounge will seat a whole party at the
same time, I call my lounge *Party Lounge*." (Frederick Kiesler, 1939)

Wittmann Möbelwerkstätten
Re-Edition Friedrich Kiesler
Correalistische Möbel
Bed Couch
Party Lounge

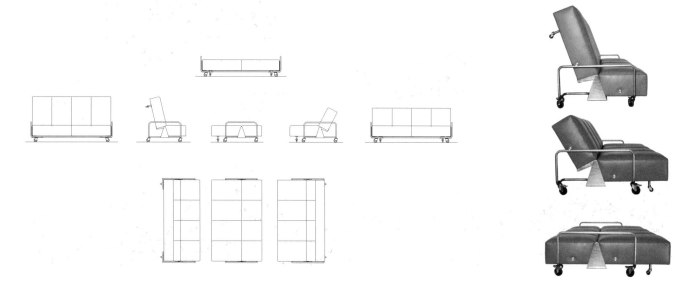

Bed Couch

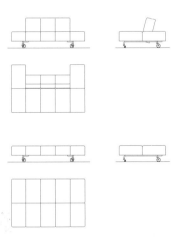

Party Lounge

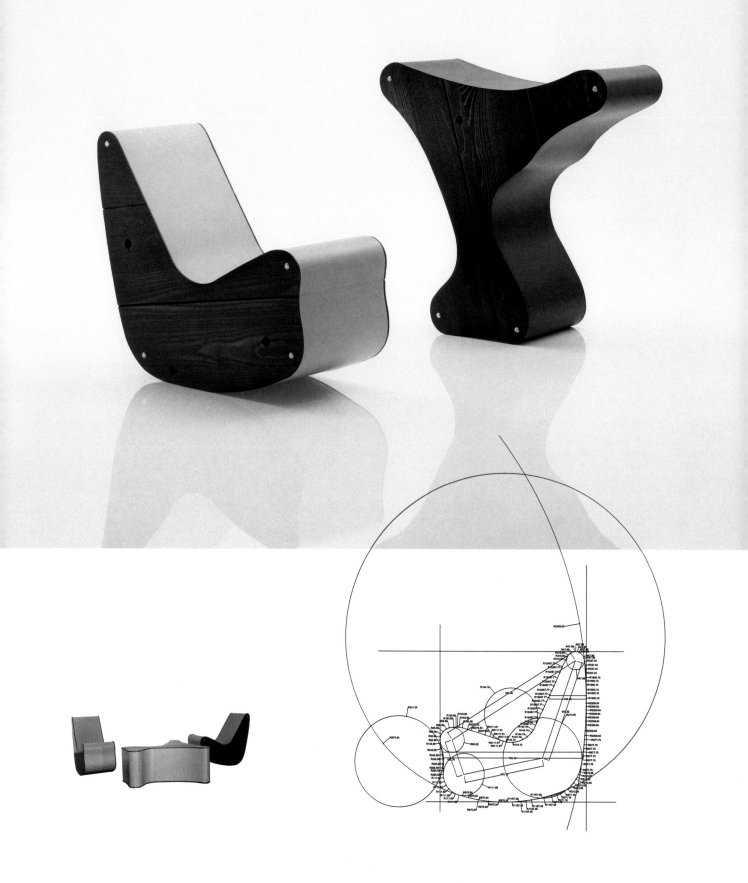

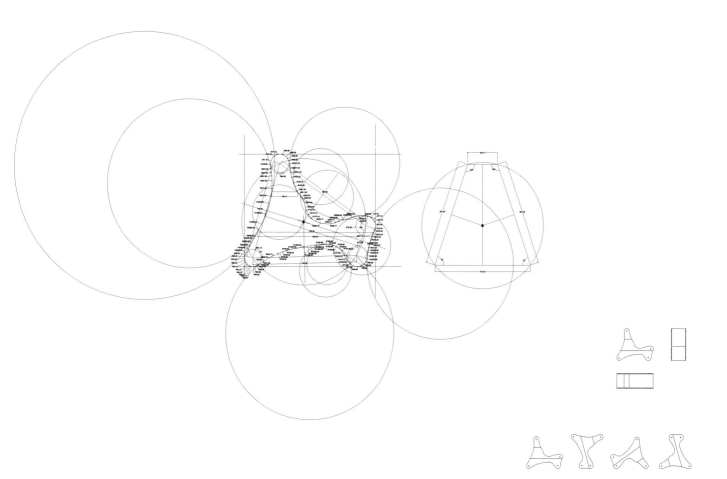

Correalistisches Instrument
Correalist Instrument

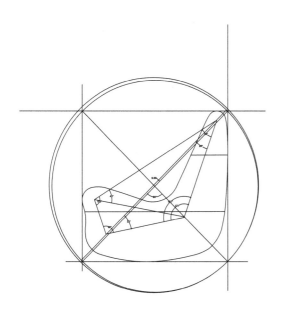

Correalistischer Rocker
Correalist Rocker

Anhang
Appendix

Biografie

Biography

Friedrich Kiesler 1890-1965

Zusammengestellt von Valentina Sonzogni

Die hier angeführten biografischen Daten sind folgenden Publikationen entnommen: *Peggy Guggenheim & Frederick Kiesler. The Story of Art of This Century*, hrsg. von Susan Davidson und Philip Rylands, Ausst.-Kat. Peggy Guggenheim Collection Venice, Ostfildern 2004 and *Friedrich Kiesler 1890-1965*, hrsg. von Dieter Bogner, Ausst.-Kat. Museum für Moderne Kunst Stiftung Ludwig Wien, Wien 1988.

1890-1923
Friedrich Jakob Kiesler wird am 22. September 1890 in Czernowitz, Rumänien, als Sohn von Julius Kiesler und Maria Meister geboren. 1908 übersiedelt er nach Wien, wo er an der K. K. Wiener Technischen Hochschule sowie an der Akademie der bildenden Künste Architektur studiert. 1920 ehelicht Kiesler in der Wiener Synagoge die Philologiestudentin Stephanie „Steffi" Frischer (geb. 1897).

1924
24. September-12. Oktober In den 20er Jahren kreiert Kiesler innovative Entwürfe für das Theater sowie Ausstellungsinstallationen in Wien und Berlin. Im Rahmen der „Internationalen Ausstellung Neuer Theatertechnik" in Wien realisiert er die *Raumbühne* sowie das *L+T System*, ein Ausstellungsmöbel für die Präsentation von Kunstwerken, Büchern und anderen Ausstellungsstücken.

1925
28. April-7. November Auf Einladung von Josef Hoffmann übersiedeln Friedrich Kiesler und seine Frau Steffi für die Gestaltung der Theatersektion des Österreichischen Pavillons im Rahmen der Pariser „Exposition International des Arts Décoratifs et Industriels Modernes" in die französische Hauptstadt. Kiesler entwirft die Installation *Raumstadt* als Modell einer schwebenden Stadt der Zukunft als Display für Theatermodelle. Während seines Aufenthalts in Paris entwirft er zwei horizontale Hochhäuser und zeichnet einige städteplanerische Entwürfe für den Place de la Concorde.

1926
26. März Auf Einladung von Jane Heap, Herausgeberin der avantgardistischen Zeitschrift *The Little Review*, treffen Friedrich und Steffi Kiesler in New York ein um die „International Theatre Exposition" im Steinway Building zu installieren. Im Rahmen dieser Ausstellung stellt Kiesler das Modell eines *Endless Theater* mit zwei Plänen für eine spiralförmige Bühne vor.
11. November-1. Jänner 1927 Im Brooklyn Museum in New York findet die von Katherine S. Dreier und ihrer Société Anonyme organisierte „International Exhibition of Modern Art" statt. Kiesler entwirft für diese Ausstellung einen *Television Room* mit Schiebewänden und Projektionen von klassischen Kunstwerken, seine Pläne werden jedoch nicht umgesetzt.

1927
Kiesler gestaltet das *Theatre for Brooklyn Heights*, bestehend aus zwei Zuschauerräumen und einer runden Bühne in der Mitte. Von nun an findet sich auf seinen Briefen der Briefkopf „frederick kiesler architect new york, 64 west 49th street". Dank seiner Bekanntschaft mit Katherine S. Dreier tritt er mit Harvey Wiley Corbett in Verbindung, um Erkundigungen über die Architekturbranche in den Vereinigten Staaten einzuholen.

1928
Für das Kaufhaus Saks Fifth Avenue in New York entwirft Kiesler Schaufensterauslagen in modernistischem Stil. Er entwickelt eine neue Präsentationsmethode, die auf konstruktivistischen Formen und industriellen Materialien sowie einer dramaturgischen Lichtführung beruht.
Mai Simon Gould, Direktor der Film Arts Guild, beauftragt Kiesler mit der Gestaltung eines Kinotheaters in Greenwich Village. In dieser Zeit tritt Kiesler der neu gegründeten Designervereinigung *AUDAC* (American Union of Decorative Arts and Craftsmen) bei. Die erste Ausstellung dieser Gruppe findet 1930 statt.

1929
1. Februar Kieslers *Film Guild Cinema* in der 52 West 8th Street in New York wird eröffnet. Das Projekt stellt seinen ersten abgeschlossenen Auftrag in den Vereinigten Staaten dar. Das Theater erhält Beifall für den flexiblen Rahmen der Projektionsfläche, der sich wie eine Iris öffnet und schließt. Für die Möblierung des Kinos zeichnet Ilonka Karasz verantwortlich.

Frederick Kiesler 1890-1965

Compiled by Valentina Sonzogni

The following biographical facts are taken from: *Peggy Guggenheim & Frederick Kiesler. The Story of Art of This Century*, ed. by Susan Davidson und Philip Rylands, exh. cat. Peggy Guggenheim Collection Venice, Ostfildern 2004 and *Friedrich Kiesler 1890-1965*, ed. by Dieter Bogner, exhibition catalogue, Museum für Moderne Kunst Stiftung Ludwig Wien, Wien 1988.

1890-1923
Friedrich Jacob Kiesler is born on September 22, 1890 in Cernauti, Romania, son of Julius Kiesler and Maria Meister. In 1908 he moves to Vienna to study architecture at the K. K. Wiener Technische Hochschule and in the Akademie der bildenden Künste. In 1920 Kiesler marries Stephanie "Steffi" Frischer (born 1897), a student of philology, in the Vienna Synagogue.

1924
September 24-October 12 During the 1920s, he produces innovative theater designs and exhibition installations in Vienna and Berlin, including the "Internationale Ausstellung Neuer Theatertechnik" in Vienna, for which he designs the *Raumbühne* and the *L+T-System*, an exhibition furniture unit for displaying art works as well as books and other exhibits.

1925
April 28 – November 7 Invited by Josef Hoffmann, Kiesler and Steffi move to Paris to design the theatre section of the Austrian Pavilion at the "Exposition International des Arts Décoratifs et Industriels Modernes", in Paris. He realizes the installation *City in Space* as a prototype of a future suspended city which functions as an exhibition display for theatre models. While in Paris, he designs two horizontal skyscrapers and draws some urban development plans for Place de la Concorde.

1926
March 26 Invited by Jane Heap, editor of the avant-garde magazine *The Little Review*, Frederick Kiesler and his wife Steffi arrive in New York to install the "International Theatre Exposition" at the Steinway Building. In this exhibition, he presents a model of an *Endless Theater* with two plans of a spiral stage.
November 11-January 1, 1927 The "International Exhibition of Modern Art", organized by Katherine S. Dreier and her Société Anonyme, is held at the Brooklyn Museum, New York. For this exhibition, Kiesler designs a *Television Room* with sliding panels and projections of classic art works, although the plans are not realized.

1927
Kiesler designs the *Theatre for Brooklyn Heights* composed of two auditoriums and of a round stage in the middle. He starts to write his letters on paper with letterhead: "frederick kiesler architect new york, 64 west 49th street". Thanks to his acquaintance with Katherine S. Dreier he makes contact with Harvey Wiley Corbett to gather information on the architecture business in the U.S.

1928
Kiesler designs modernist window displays for Saks Fifth Avenue, New York. He develops a new presentation method using constructivist forms and industrial materials as well as a dramatic use of light.
May Simon Gould, director of the Film Arts Guild, commissions Kiesler to design a cinema theater in the Greenwich Village. In this period, Kiesler joins the newly founded *AUDAC* (American Union of Decorative Arts and Craftsmen). The first show of the group will take place in 1930.

1929
February 1 Kiesler's *Film Guild Cinema* opens at 52 West 8th Street, New York. It marks his first completed commission in the United States. The theater receives acclaim for its flexible screen frame which opens and closes like an iris. Furnishing for the cinema is designed by Ilonka Karasz.

1930

5. März Kiesler erhält die Architekturlizenz des Staates New York und gründet 1934 unter dem Namen Planners Institute Inc. seine eigene Firma. Im selben Jahr veröffentlicht er das Buch *Contemporary Art Applied to the Store and Its Display*.
März Die Ausstellung „Home Show" unter der Schirmherrschaft der *AUDAC* wird im Grand Central Palace in New York eröffnet. Kiesler möbliert einen Raum mit zwei Lehnsesseln und einem niedrigen Tisch, mit dem *Flying Desk* sowie mit einem weiteren Schreibtisch.
12. August-18. Oktober Kiesler und Steffi reisen nach Paris, um Theo und Petro „Nelly" van Doesburg zu besuchen und den Kontakt mit anderen europäischen Künstlern wie Piet Mondrian, Fernand Léger, Jean Arp, Tristan Tzara und Edgard Varèse wieder aufzunehmen.

1931

Jänner Kiesler besucht Vorlesungen an der New School for Social Research, wo er Richard Neutra, Alexander Calder, Frank Lloyd Wright u. a. begegnet.
März Einige von Kiesler entworfene Lampen werden in *Architectural Record* veröffentlicht. Vorbereitungen für einen Wettbewerb für ein Theater in Woodstock. Im Winter gewinnt Kiesler den Wettbewerb, an dem unter anderem auch Frank Lloyd Wright teilnimmt. Das Projekt sollte aus Geldmangel jedoch nie realisiert werden.

1932

Jänner Kiesler hält einen Vortrag mit dem Titel „Ornament and Crime" nach einem Aufsatz von Adolf Loos.
10. Februar-23. März Kiesler ist mit Fotografien des *Film Guild Cinema* in der Ausstellung „Modern Architecture: International Exhibition" im Museum of Modern Art vertreten, in der zeitgenössische europäische und amerikanische Architektur präsentiert wird.

1933

Jänner Kiesler hält in Grand Rapids und Chicago Vorträge über modernes Design in den Vereinigten Staaten.
Juni Kiesler reist regelmäßig nach Chicago, wo er sich nicht nur mit der Firma Sears & Roebuck trifft, in der Hoffnung, sein *Nucleus House* zu realisieren, sondern auch mit der Rembrandt Lamp Corporation, für die er Beleuchtungssysteme entwirft.
August Kiesler legt dem Patentamt „Perspective View of Flexible Partition Room" vor, ein frühes Konzept für die Innengestaltung des *Space House*.
Herbst Kiesler beginnt mit der Gestaltung von Bühnenbildern für Theater und Oper für die Juilliard School of Music in New York, an der er auch bis 1957 lehrt.
16. Oktober In der Modernage Furniture Company, 162 East 33rd Street, New York, wird der Prototyp des *Space House* eröffnet. Als Einfamilienhaus ohne Innenwände konzipiert, die durch bewegliche Trennwände aus Gummi ersetzt werden, wird es mit Stücken von Gilbert Rhode und anderen Designern ausgestattet.

1934

Jänner Kiesler hält im Rahmen der großen Möbelmesse Merchandise Mart zwei Vorträge in Chicago. Er spricht zum Thema „The Difference Between Good and Bad Modern Design" und konzentriert sich dabei vor allem auf den Unterschied zwischen funktionalen und biotechnischen Ansätzen bei der Produkt- und Innenraumgestaltung.
Juni Kiesler plant ein American Institute for Industrial Design, das als gemeinschaftlicher Lebens- und Arbeitsraum für Studenten konzipiert ist, wie in einem Artikel von E. M. Benson im American Magazine of Arts unter dem Titel „Wanted: An American Bauhaus" beschrieben.
15. September Das von Kiesler 1930 gegründete Planners Institute wird als Gesellschaft eingetragen. Seit 1930 arbeitet Sidney Janis' Frau Hansi in Kieslers Büro als seine Assistentin. Im gleichen Zeitraum wird Kiesler Mitglied des Designbüros WPA/FAP (Works Progress Administration Federal Art Project) mit William Lescaze, Meyer Schapiro und Alfred Auerbach.
Oktober Kiesler legt dem Patentamt Pläne für ein Projekt mit dem Namen *Floor & Ceiling Plan of a Television Auditorium* vor, um es urheberrechtlich schützen zu lassen.

1935

Kiesler übernimmt die Gestaltung von Jay's Shoe Shop in Buffalo, N. Y., wofür er einen Preis für das beste Ladendesign gewinnt, und entwirft den Westermann Bookstore in New York City. Darüber hinaus arbeitet er an der Gestaltung einer ganzen Wohnzimmereinrichtung für das Apartment der Textildesignerin Marguerite „Alma" Mergentime.
Sommer Der Kunstsammler Walter Arensberg kontaktiert Kiesler und beauftragt ihn mit der Planung eines Einfamilienhauses. Kiesler lehnt den Auftrag mit der Begründung ab, er entwerfe nur Dinge, die er auch noch im Produktionsstadium kontrollieren könne.
Im **September** übersiedeln die Kieslers in ein Penthouse in der 7th Avenue Nr. 56, wo sie bis zu Kieslers Tod wohnen werden.

1930

March 5 Kiesler receives his architect's license from the State of New York and in 1934 establishes his firm, the Planners Institute Inc. During the year, he publishes the book *Contemporary Art Applied to the Store and Its Display*.
March The exhibition "Home Show" under the auspices of the *AUDAC* opens at Grand Central Palace in New York. Kiesler furnishes a room with two armchairs and a low table; with the *Flying Desk* and with an additional desk.
August 12-October 18 Kiesler and Steffi travel to Paris, visiting Theo and Petro "Nelly" van Doesburg, as well as renewing contact with other European artists, such as Piet Mondrian, Fernand Léger, Jean Arp, Tristan Tzara, and Edgard Varèse.

1931

January Kiesler attends lectures at the New School for Social Research, where he meets with Richard Neutra, Alexander Calder, Frank Lloyd Wright, a. o.
March Some lamps designed by Kiesler are published in *Architectural Record*. He prepares a competition for a theater in Woodstock. In winter he wins the competition in which, among others, Frank Lloyd Wright takes part. The project will never be realized due to lack of funds.

1932

January Kiesler holds a lecture titled "Ornament and Crime" after the essay by Adolf Loos.
February 10-March 23 Kiesler is represented with photographs of the *Film Guild Cinema* in "Modern Architecture: International Exhibition" at the Museum of Modern Art and including contemporary European and American architecture.

1933

January Kiesler holds a lecture on modern American design in Grand Rapids and Chicago.
June Kiesler travels regularly to Chicago where he meets not only with Sears & Roebuck, with whom he hopes to realize his *Nucleus House*, but also with the Rembrandt Lamp Corporation for which he designs lighting systems.
August Kiesler delivers to the copyright office a "Perspective View of Flexible Partition Room", an early idea for the interior design of the *Space House*.
Autumn Kiesler begins designing theater and opera sets for the Juilliard School of Music, New York, where he also teaches until 1957.
October 16 The prototype of the *Space House* opens in the Modernage Furniture Company, 162 East 33rd Street, New York. Conceived as a detached family house in which the interior walls are replaced by movable rubber partitions, the house is furnished with pieces by Gilbert Rhode and other designers.

1934

January Kiesler holds two lectures in Chicago in a large furniture fair, the Merchandise Mart. He lectures on the theme "The Difference Between Good and Bad Modern Design" focusing on the difference between a functional and a biotechnical approach to the design of product and interior design.
June Kiesler plans an American Institute for Industrial Design, conceived as a communal space for students' life and work, as reported by E. M. Benson in the American Magazine of Arts in an article titled "Wanted: An American Bauhaus."
September 15 The Planners Institute that Kiesler founded in 1930 is incorporated. Sidney Janis's wife, Hansi, has been working in Kiesler's office as his assistant since 1930. In the same period he becomes a member of the WPA/FAP (Works Progress Administration Federal Art Project) Design Studio with William Lescaze, Meyer Schapiro and Alfred Auerbach.
October Kiesler delivers to the copyright office plans for a project titled *Floor & Ceiling Plan of a Television Auditorium*.

1935

Kiesler designs Jay's Shoes Shop in Buffalo, N.Y. for which he wins a prize for the best shop design, and Westermann Bookstore in New York City. He also works on the design of a whole living room for the apartment of the fabric designer Marguerite "Alma" Mergentime.
Summer The art collector Walter Arensberg contacts Kiesler and commissions him to create plans for a detached family house. Kiesler declines explaining that he does not design anything unless he can control even the construction phase.
In **September** the Kieslers move to the Penthouse at 56, 7th Avenue, which will remain their address until Kiesler's death.

1936
Kiesler erhält die amerikanische Staatsbürgerschaft.
Jänner Kiesler legt Zeichnungen für die Patentierung einer *Party Lounge & Furniture Construction* sowie später einer *Lamp and Table Construction* vor.
2. März-19. April Kieslers Bühnengestaltung für *R.U.R.* und *Emperor Jones* sowie ein Foto von der *Raumbühne* und eine Stehlampe sind Teil der von Alfred H. Barr im Museum of Modern Art organisierten Ausstellung „Cubism and Abstract Art".
Juni Kiesler stellt die Einrichtung für das Mergentime-Apartment fertig.
Dezember Kiesler erhält das Angebot, Sommerkurse an der Columbia University sowie im Winter einen Lehrgang für Bühnengestaltung in Zusammenarbeit mit der Juilliard School of Music zu organisieren.

1937
Februar Kiesler beginnt mit der Veröffentlichung einer Reihe von Artikeln zum Thema „Design Correlation" in der Zeitschrift *Architectural Record*. Im Mai publiziert er einen Beitrag zu Marcel Duchamps *La Mariée mise à nu par ses célibataires, même* und erhält dafür einen lobenden Brief von Duchamp.
Juli Kiesler wird zum „Associate in Architecture" an der Columbia University ernannt und hält dort einen Sommerkurs über Möbeldesign.
Herbst Kiesler gründet das *Laboratory for Design Correlation* an der Fakultät für Architektur der Columbia University in New York, um die dynamischen Wechselbeziehungen zwischen Design und Lebensprozessen zu untersuchen. Daneben nimmt er die Arbeit an der *Vision Machine* (1937-41) auf.
13. Dezember Mies van der Rohe besucht Kieslers Penthouse, wo ihn Kiesler auf der Terrasse fotografiert.

1938
Frühjahr Gemeinsam mit Studenten des *Laboratory for Design Correlation* arbeitet Kiesler an dem Projekt *Mobile Home Library*.
Juni Er hält erneut einen Sommerkurs an der Columbia University und spricht in einem Symposium am MIT zum Thema *Biotechnique versus Architecture*.

1939
September Kiesler veröffentlicht „On Correalism and Biotechnique: A Definition and Test of a New Approach to Building Design" in der Zeitschrift *Architectural Record*.

1940
Februar Kiesler hält im Rahmen der Ann Arbor Conference for Design einen Vortrag zum Thema „Architecture as Biotechnique". Während der folgenden Monate hält er Vorlesungen am Teachers College und an der Yale University.

1941
Juni Das *Laboratory for Design Correlation* wird aus budgetären Gründen geschlossen.

1942
21. Oktober Die Galerie *Art of This Century*, die Kiesler im Laufe von neun Monaten für die Kunstsammlung von Peggy Guggenheim entworfen hat, wird eröffnet. Bereits nach kurzer Zeit entwickelt sich das Museum/die Galerie zu einem Treffpunkt für Künstler, Kritiker, Studenten, Sammler und Persönlichkeiten aus der Kulturszene. Neben dem Gesamtkonzept und dem Beleuchtungssystem entwirft Kiesler ein *Correalistisches Instrument* in drei unterschiedlichen Varianten, einen zusammenklappbaren Stuhl sowie ein Präsentationsmöbel für Gemälde.

1943
Duchamp entwirft den Umschlag für *VVV* Almanac for 1943 (Nr. 2-3). In Zusammenarbeit mit Kiesler gestaltet er die Rückseite als gestanztes Profil eines weiblichen Torsos mit Hühnerdraht „Twin-Touch-Test". In derselben Ausgabe erscheint auch Kieslers „Design Correlation as an Approach to Architectural Planning, Art of This Century Galleries, New York".

1944
Sommer Kiesler trifft mit dem Bauhaus-Typografen und Designer Herbert Bayer sowie mit Albert E. Parr, dem Direktor des American Museum of Natural History, zusammen, vermutlich um die Gestaltung einer Ausstellung für das Museum zu besprechen, die jedoch nicht umgesetzt wird. Zur selben Zeit kreiert Kiesler im Auftrag des Architekten Harvey Wiley Corbett Gouache-Entwürfe für eine Ausstellung amerikanischer Architektur in Moskau. Die Ausstellung wird im Winter 1945 in reduzierter, modularer Form eröffnet.
Herbst László Moholy-Nagy lädt Kiesler ein, in Chicago Vorträge zum Thema „The Problems of Design Correlation in Nature and Technology" zu halten.

1945
12. Dezember 1944-31. Jänner Kiesler entwirft das Beleuchtungssystem für die von Duchamp organisierte und in der Julien Levy Gallery in New York

1936
Kiesler obtains the American citizenship.
January Kiesler delivers drawings to patent a *Party Lounge & Furniture Construction* and later a *Lamp and Table Construction*.
March 2-April 19 Kiesler's theater design for *R.U.R.* and *Emperor Jones* as well as a photo of the *Raumbühne* (*Space Stage*) and a floor lamp are included in the exhibition "Cubism and Abstract Art" organized by Alfred H. Barr at the Museum of Modern Art.
June Kiesler completes the furnishing of the Mergentime apartment.
December Kiesler receives the offer to organize summer courses at Columbia University and a course in stage design in cooperation with the Juilliard School of Music in winter.

1937
February Kiesler starts to publish a series of articles on the theme of "Design Correlation" in the magazine *Architectural Record*. In May he publishes a feature on Marcel Duchamps, *La Mariée mise à nu par ses célibataires, même*, eventually receiving a letter of praise by Duchamp.
July He is appointed "Associate in Architecture" at Columbia University and holds a summer course on furniture design.
Autumn Kiesler establishes the *Laboratory for Design Correlation* at the School of Architecture at Columbia University, New York, in order to study the dynamic interaction of design with life processes. He begins working on the *Vision Machine* (1937-41).
December 13 Mies van der Rohe visits Kiesler's Penthouse and Kiesler takes a picture of him on the terrace.

1938
Spring Kiesler works on the *Mobile Home Library*, a project in cooperation with the students of the *Laboratory for Design Correlation*.
June He holds another summer course at Columbia University and speaks at MIT in a symposium on the theme of *Biotechnique versus Architecture*.

1939
September Kiesler publishes "On Correalism and Biotechnique: A Definition and Test of a New Approach to Building Design" in *Architectural Record*.

1940
February Kiesler lectures at Ann Arbor Conference for Design with a paper titled "Architecture as Biotechnique". During the following months he lectures at the Teachers College and at Yale University.

1941
June The *Laboratory for Design Correlation* is closed down for budgetary reasons.

1942
October 21 *Art of This Century*, the gallery that Kiesler spent nine months designing for Peggy Guggenheim's art collection, opens to the public. The museum/gallery quickly becomes a meeting place for artists, critics, students, collectors, and a range of cultural personalities. Besides the overall concept and the lighting system, Kiesler designs a *Correalist Instrument* in three different variations, a foldable stool, and a display stand for paintings.

1943
Duchamp designs the cover for *VVV* Almanac for 1943 (nos. 2-3). With Kiesler's collaboration, the back cover design is a die-cut of the profile of a woman's torso containing chicken wire, the "Twin-Touch-Test". Kiesler's "Design Correlation as an Approach to Architectural Planning, Art of This Century Galleries, New York" appears in the same issue.

1944
Summer Kiesler meets Bauhaus typographer and designer Herbert Bayer and Albert E. Parr, director of the American Museum of Natural History, probably to discuss designing an exhibition for the museum which was ultimately not built. At the same time, on behalf of the architect Harvey Wiley Corbett, Kiesler creates gouache designs for an exhibition of American architecture in Moscow. The exhibition opens in the winter of 1945 in a reduced modular.
Autumn László Moholy-Nagy invites Kiesler to lecture in Chicago on the subject of "The Problems of Design Correlation in Nature and Technology".

1945
December 12, 1944-January 31 Kiesler designs the lighting system for "The Imagery of Chess: A Group Exhibition of Painting, Sculpture, Newly Designed

präsentierte Ausstellung „The Imagery of Chess: A Group Exhibition of Painting, Sculpture, Newly Designed Chessmen, Music, and Miscellany".
Dezember Das Planners Institute Inc. wird wegen Nichtzahlung von Steuern geschlossen.

1946
Winter Kiesler veröffentlicht „Art and Architecture: Notes on the Spiral Theme in Recent Architecture" in der Zeitschrift *Partisan Review*. Der Text enthält eine Analyse von Frank Lloyd Wrights Plänen für das Museum of Non-Objective Painting.
Sommer Fertigstellung seines in den späten 30er Jahren begonnenen Buches *Magic Architecture*, das jedoch nie einen Verleger finden sollte.

1947
3. März „Bloodflames 1947", eine von Kiesler gestaltete Ausstellung, wird in der Hugo Gallery in New York vorgestellt. Kontinuierliche biomorphe Farbmuster auf Boden, Decke und Wänden verwandeln die Galerie. Kiesler verwendet einige *Correalistische Instrumente* aus *Art of This Century* als Mobiliar für die Galerie. Er schlägt Wallace K. Harrison vor, die Einrichtung für dessen RCA Building, Rockefeller Center zu gestalten.
8. Juli-5. Oktober Die von Duchamp und Breton organisierte und von Kiesler gestaltete Ausstellung „Exposition Internationale du Surréalisme" wird in der Galerie Maeght, Paris, präsentiert. Mit *Totem for All Religions* (1947, umgesetzt von Étienne Martin) und *Anti-Taboo Figure* (1947) umfasst die Schau unter anderem auch zwei skulpturale Werke von Kiesler. In Paris entwickelt er erstmals die Idee zum *Endless House* und zeichnet erste Entwürfe.

1948
April Kiesler arbeitet an einem *Galaxial portrait* von Wilfredo Lam und organisiert die Schaufenstergestaltung für die Zeitschrift *NEON* im Rahmen der Gotham Book Mart.
29. Juli Kiesler sendet das fertige Manuskript des „Manifeste du Corréalisme", seines bahnbrechenden Textes über Architektur, Kunst und Design, an André Bloc.

1949
Juni Bloc veröffentlicht das „Manifeste du Corréalisme" in L'architecture d'aujourd'hui. Diese 1947 verfasste Theorie einer Vereinigung der Künste präsentiert Kieslers bedeutendste Projekte in den Bereichen Architektur und Ausstellungsdesign.
Juli „Pseudo-Functionalism in Modern Architecture" wird in der Zeitschrift *Partisan Review* veröffentlicht.

1950
Oktober Das erste Modell des *Endless House* ist Teil der Ausstellung „The Muralist and the Modern Architects" in der Kootz Gallery in New York, die Gemeinschafts-arbeiten von Künstlern und Architekten zeigt.

1951
Jänner CBS wählt Kiesler zum „Architect of the Year".
Juni Das Museum of Modern Art erwirbt das kleine Modell des *Endless House* sowie einige dazugehörige Zeichnungen, die erstmals in der Ausstellung in der Kootz Gallery präsentiert wurden.

1952
April Kieslers *Galaxy* ist Teil von Dorothy Millers Ausstellung „Fifteen Americans".

1953
Sommer Eine für das Haus von Philip Johnson in New Canaan, Connecticut, konzipierte *Galaxy* wird fertiggestellt und im Freien installiert. Die Skulptur wird 1956 durch Blitzschlag zerstört.

1954
27. September-19. Oktober Die Sidney Janis Gallery zeigt in ihrer ersten Einzelausstellung gemalte *Galaxies*.

1955
16. Jänner-6. Februar Kieslers *Galaxies* werden im Museum of Fine Arts in Houston ausgestellt. Er selbst verbringt den Monat August in Frankreich, wo er an Tonskulpturen arbeitet.
3. August Das *Endless Theater*, entworfen für das Empire State Music Festival in Ellenville, New York, als Zelt für 2000 Zuseher, wird mit Shakespeares „Der Sturm" eröffnet.

1956
Kiesler zeichnet im Auftrag von Paul Tishman Pläne für einen Wohnblock am Washington Square sowie für das Steifel Building, beide Entwürfe sollten jedoch

Chessmen, Music, and Miscellany", organized by Duchamp and presented at Julien Levy Gallery, New York.
December The Planners Institute Inc. is closed due to non-payment of taxes.

1946
Winter Kiesler publishes "Art and Architecture: Notes on the Spiral Theme in Recent Architecture" in *Partisan Review*. The text includes an analysis of Frank Lloyd Wright's plans for the Museum of Non-Objective Painting.
Summer Kiesler completes his book *Magic Architecture*, begun in the late 1930s; a publisher is never found.

1947
March 3 "Bloodflames 1947", an exhibition designed by Kiesler, is presented at Hugo Gallery, New York. The gallery is transformed by applying continuous painted biomorphic patterns on the floor, walls, and ceiling. He uses some *Correalist Instruments* from *Art of This Century* as furniture for the gallery. He proposes to Wallace K. Harrison to design the furniture of his RCA Building at the Rockefeller Center.
July 8-October 5 "Exposition Internationale du Surréalisme", organized by Duchamp and Breton and designed by Kiesler, is presented at Galerie Maeght, Paris. The exhibition includes two sculptural works by Kiesler, *Totem for All Religions* (1947, realized by Étienne Martin) and *Anti-Taboo Figure* (1947). In Paris, he first conceives and starts preliminary sketches for the *Endless House*.

1948
April Kiesler works on a *Galaxial portrait* of Wilfredo Lam and organizes the window display for *NEON* Magazine at Gotham Book Mart.
July 29 He sends to André Bloc the finished manuscript of his seminal text on architecture, arts and design "Manifeste du Corréalisme".

1949
June Bloc publishes "Manifeste du Corréalisme" in *L'architecture d'aujourd'hui*. Kiesler's theory of the unified arts (written in 1947) presents Kiesler's most significant projects in the fields of architecture and exhibition design.
July "Pseudo-Functionalism in Modern Architecture" is published in *Partisan Review*.

1950
October The first model of the *Endless House* is included in the exhibition "The Muralist and the Modern Architects" at the Kootz Gallery in New York, featuring the combined work of artists and architects.

1951
January CBS elects Kiesler "Architect of the Year".
June The Museum of Modern Art purchases the small *Endless House* model and some related drawings, which were first included in the show at the Kootz Gallery.

1952
April Kiesler's *Galaxy* is included in Dorothy Miller's show "Fifteen Americans".

1953
Summer Kiesler completes and installs an outdoor *Galaxy* for the house of Philip Johnson at New Canaan, Connecticut. The sculpture will be destroyed by lightning in 1956.

1954
September 27-October 19 The Sidney Janis Gallery shows painted *Galaxies* in its first one-artist exhibition.

1955
January 16-February 6 Kiesler's *Galaxies* are shown in the Museum of Fine Arts in Houston. He spends the month of August in France, working on clay sculptures.
August 3 *The Endless Theater* designed as a tent for 2000 spectators for the Empire State Music Festival in Ellenville, New York, opens with Shakespeare's "The Tempest".

1956
Kiesler draws plans for an apartment house in Washington Square and for the Steifel Building. Both were commissioned by Paul Tishman and both

nie umgesetzt werden. Weiters plant er ein zehnstöckiges Gebäude für John Jacob Astor in West Palm Beach.

1957
22. Dezember Gemeinsam mit Armand Bartos arbeitet Kiesler an der Gestaltung der *World House Gallery*, die sich über zwei Stockwerke des Carlyle Hotels an der Ecke Madison Avenue und 76th Street in New York erstreckt. Das Ergebnis dieser Arbeit – geschwungene Wände, eine abgehängte Treppe mit verglasten Seitenwänden, eingebaute Pflanzengefäße rund um ein großes Wasserbecken etc. – wird von den Kritikern sehr positiv aufgenommen. Kiesler arbeitet an der Rekonstruktion eines maurisch-venezianischen Theaters in Caramoor, Katonah, New York und zeichnet Pläne für ein Haus von Karl Robbins in West Palm Beach und für ein Haus von Benjamin Javitz.

1958
Kiesler erhält finanzielle Unterstützung für die Realisierung von ersten Entwürfen für ein *Endless House*, das im Garten des Museum of Modern Art in New York gebaut werden soll, und nimmt die Arbeit an den *Shell Sculptures* auf.

1959
Kiesler arbeitet gemeinsam mit Armand Bartos an der architektonischen Gestaltung für das Ullman Research Center for Health and Science an der Yeshiva University in New York. Während dieser Zeit werden verschiedene Teile und Modelle für das *Endless House* gebaut.

1960
Kiesler erhält ein Stipendium von der Ford Foundation für Studien und ein Modell für ein *Universal Theatre* im Rahmen eines Wettbewerbs zum Thema „The Ideal Theatre: Eight Concepts". Das Museum of Modern Art zeigt in der Ausstellung „Visionary Architecture" ein großes Modell des *Endless House*.

1961
Einzelausstellung der *Shell Sculptures* und *Galaxies* in der Leo Castelli Gallery. Kiesler verhandelt mit Mary Sisler über den Bau eines *Endless House* in Palm Beach, Florida. Reisen nach Rom und Israel.

1962
Kiesler entwickelt zahlreiche Entwürfe und einige Modelle für eine *Grotto for Meditation* für Jane Owen in New Harmony, Indiana.

1963
Kiesler nimmt die große Environmental Sculpture *US-YOU-ME* in Angriff und stellt Tagebuchnotizen und andere Schriften für *Inside the Endless House* zusammen. Dieses Buch seiner Erinnerungen wird 1966 posthum von Simon & Schuster veröffentlicht werden.
3. September Steffi Kiesler stirbt.

1964
26. März Kiesler heiratet Lillian Olinsey. Arbeitet an seiner Skulptur *Bucephalus*.

1965
27. Dezember Kiesler stirbt an Herzversagen. Zwei Tage später wird im Beerdigungsinstitut Frank E. Campbell Funeral Home, 1076 Madison Avenue, New York, eine Trauerfeier in Form einer Performance abgehalten. Der Dichter e. e. cummings, MoMA-Direktor René d'Harnoncourt, der Dramatiker Sidney Kingsley, der Textildesigner Jack Leonore Larsen und der Komponist Virgil Thomson halten Lobreden. In Hommage an Kiesler rollt der Künstler Robert Rauschenberg einen Reifen durch den Mittelgang und bemalt diesen. Auch der Tänzer Eric Hawkins hält vor dem Sarg Kieslers eine Performance. Das Juilliard String Quartet spielt Musik von Mozart und Schönberg.

were never built. Furthermore he conceives a ten-story building for John Jacob Astor in West Palm Beach.

1957
December 22 Kiesler collaborates with Armand Bartos to design the *World House Gallery* on two floors of the Carlyle Hotel, Madison Avenue at 76th Street, New York. The design – featuring curved walls, a suspended glass-enclosed staircase, and the verdant built-in foliage planters around a large pool of water – is the subject of much positive critical commentary. Kiesler works on the reconstruction of a Moorish-Venetian theatre at Caramoor in Katonah, New York and draws plans of a house for Karl Robbins in West Palm Beach and of a house for Benjamin Javitz.

1958
Kiesler receives a grant for the realization of preliminary sketches for an *Endless House* to be built in the garden of the Museum of Modern Art in New York and starts working on the *Shell Sculptures*.

1959
He works with Armand Bartos on the architectural design for the Ullman Research Center for Health and Science at the Yeshiva University in New York. In this period several segments and models for the *Endless House* are built.

1960
Kiesler receives a grant from the Ford Foundation for studies and a model of a *Universal Theatre* for a competition on the theme "The Ideal Theatre: Eight Concepts". The Museum of Modern Art shows a large model of the *Endless House* in the exhibition "Visionary Architecture".

1961
One-man show of *Shell Sculptures* and *Galaxies* at the Leo Castelli Gallery. Kiesler negotiates with Mary Sisler for the construction of an *Endless House* in Palm Beach, Florida. Travels to Rome and Israel.

1962
Kiesler develops numerous sketches and some models for a *Grotto for Meditation* for Jane Owen in New Harmony, Indiana.

1963
Kiesler begins the large environmental sculpture *US-YOU-ME* and assembles journal notes and other writings for *Inside the Endless House*, a book of his recollections published posthumously in 1966 by Simon & Schuster.
September 3 Steffi Kiesler dies.

1964
March 26 Kiesler marries Lillian Olinsey. Works on his sculpture *Bucephalus*.

1965
December 27 Kiesler dies of heart failure. A memorial service, in the form of a performance event, is held two days later at Frank E. Campbell Funeral Home, 1076 Madison Avenue, New York. Eulogies are delivered by poet e. e. cummings, MoMA director René d'Harnoncourt, playwright Sidney Kingsley, textile designer Jack Leonore Larsen, and composer Virgil Thomson. As homage to Kiesler, artist Robert Rauschenberg rolls a tire down the aisle and paints it. The dancer Eric Hawkins also performs in front of Kiesler's coffin and the Juilliard String Quartet plays music by Mozart and Schönberg.

Literaturliste (Auswahl)
Bibliography (selection)

Peggy Guggenheim & Frederick Kiesler. The Story of Art of This Century. Ed. Susan Davidson and Philip Rylands. Exh. cat. Peggy Guggenheim Collection Venice. Ostfildern 2004.

Lambert, Phyllis. Mies van der Rohe in America. New York 2004.

Friedrich Kiesler, Endless House: 1947-1961. Hrsg. von der Österreichischen Friedrich und Lillian Kiesler-Privatstiftung Wien und dem MMK Museum moderner Kunst Frankfurt/Main. Ausst.-Kat. MMK Frankfurt. Ostfildern 2003.

Moravánsky, Ákos et al. Architekturtheorie im 20. Jahrhundert. Eine kritische Anthologie. Wien und New York 2003.

Friedrich Kiesler: Art of This Century, New York 1942. Hrsg. von der Österreichischen Friedrich und Lillian Kiesler-Privatstiftung Wien und dem MMK-Museum moderner Kunst Frankfurt/Main. Ausst.-Kat. MMK Frankfurt. Ostfildern 2002.

Frederick J. Kiesler – Endless Space. Ed. Dieter Bogner and Peter Noever. Exh. cat. MAK Center Los Angeles. Ostfildern 2001.

Brooks, Bruce and Robert Wojtowicz. Frank Lloyd Wright & Lewis Mumford. Thirty Years of Correspondence. New York 2001.

Eliel, Carol S. L'Esprit Nouveau, Purism in Paris 1918-1925. New York 2001.

Kennedy, David M. Freedom from Fear. New York 2001.

Steward, John J. American Modern: 1925-1940. Design for a New Age. New York 2000.

Friedrich Kiesler. Inside the Endless House. Hrsg. von Dieter Bogner. Ausst.-Kat. Historisches Museum der Stadt Wien. Wien 1997.

Hirdina, Heinz. „Die Avantgarde und der Weg nach Byzanz." Form + Zweck, 9 + 10, 1994.

Stern, Robert A. M. et al. New York 1930. Architecture and Urbanism Between the Two World Wars. New York 1994.

van Doesburg, Theo. Über Europäische Architektur, Gesammelte Aufsätze aus Het Bouwbedrijf 1924-1931. Basel 1990.

Frederick Kiesler. Ed. von Lisa Phillips. Exh. cat. Whitney Museum of American Art. New York 1989.

Friedrich Kiesler 1890-1965. Hrsg. von Dieter Bogner. Ausst.-Kat. Museum für Moderne Kunst Stiftung Ludwig Wien. Wien 1988.

Greif, Martin. Depression Modern. The Thirties Style in America. New York 1988.

Koller, Gabriele. Die Radikalisierung der Phantasie. Design aus Österreich. Salzburg und Wien 1987.

The Machine Age in America. Ed. Richard G. Wilson et al. Exh. cat. The Brooklyn Museum. New York 1986.

High Styles; Twentieth-Century American Design. Ed. Lisa Philips. Exh. cat. Whitney Museum of American Art. New York 1985.

Davies, Karen. At Home in Manhattan. Modern Decorative Arts 1925 to the Depression. New York 1983.

Creighton, Thomas H. "Kiesler's Pursuit of an Idea." Progressive Architecture, 42/7, 1961.

Born, Ernst. "New Display Techniques for 'Art of This Century' designed by Frederick Kiesler". Architectural Forum, 78/2, 1943.

Benson, E. M. "Wanted: An American Institute for Industrial Design." The American Magazine of Art. June 1934.

"Modern Design in Furniture Based on Idea of Service." The New York Sun, 1934.

"Modern Home Furnishings Talks at Mart Tonight." Chicago Journal of Commerce, January 3, 1934.

Auerbach, Alfred. "Architecture and Decoration Are Wed In 'The Space House'." Retailing, Home Furnishing Edition. October 23, 1933.

Boykin, Elizabeth. "Current Displays Afford Many Suggestions for Furnishing Pleasant Homes." New York Sun. October 23, 1933.

"Space House exhibited." New York Times, October 17, 1933.

"Space House gives a Peep into Future." NY American, October 17, 1933.

"Space House Shown." N.Y. Times, October 17, 1933.

Annual of American Design 1931. Ed. Robert L. Leonard and Richard Glassgold. New York 1931.

"We Pause to Honour: Frederick Kiesler." Advertising Arts, January 1931.

Gropius, Walter. «Section Allemande.» Exposition des Arts decoratifs. Paris 1930.

Kiesler, Frederick. Inside the Endless House. New York 1966.

Kiesler, Frederick. "Putting Design to Work." The Sunday Review of Literature, September 1, 1951.

Kiesler, Frederick. «Manifeste du Corréalisme». L'Architecture d'Aujourd'hui, 6, 1949.

Kiesler, Frederick. "Design's Bad Boy." Architectural Forum, February 1947.

Kiesler, Frederick. "On Correalism and Biotechnique. A Definition and Test of a New Approach to Building Design." Architectural Record, September 1939.

Kiesler, Frederick. "Design Correlation. Certain Data Pertaining to the Genesis of Design by Light. Part II." Architectural Record, August 1937.

Kiesler, Frederick. "Design Correlation. Certain Data Pertaining to the Genesis of Design by Light. Part I." Architectural Record, July 1937.

Kiesler, Frederick. "Design Correlation. Towards a Prefabrication of Folk Festival." Architectural Record, June 1937.

Kiesler, Frederick. "Design Correlation." Architectural Record, Mai 1937.

Kiesler, Frederick. "Design Correlation. Animals and Architecture." Architectural Record, April 1937.

Kiesler, Frederick. "The Architect in Search of ... Design Correlation; a Column on Exhibits, the Theater and the Cinema." Architectural Record, February 1937.

Kiesler, Frederick. "One Living Space Convertible into Many Rooms." Home Beautiful, January 1934.

Kiesler, Frederick. "We Are On a Threshold Of a New Era of Progressive Design." Retailing, Home Furnishings Edition, January 29, 1934.

Kiesler, Frederick. "In Memoriam: Theo van Doesburg." Shelter Magazine, 2/3, April 1932.

Kiesler, Frederick. "Notes d'Amerique." Cahiers d'Art, March 1931.

Kiesler, Frederick. "Shop Window Displays, Saks and Company." Architectural Record, 3/68, October 1930.

Kiesler, Frederick. Contemporary Art Applied to The Store and Its Display. New York 1930.

Kiesler, Friedrich. "Ménagerie des Arts Decoratifs et Industriels Modernes Paris 1925." Der Querschnitt, 5, Juli 1925.

Kiesler, Friedrich. „Vitalbau – Raumstadt – Funktionelle Architektur." NB De Stijl, 10/11, 6, 1925.

Nach seinem Umzug in die USA (1926) publizierte Friedrich Kiesler unter dem Namen „Frederick Kiesler".

After his move to the USA (1926) Friedrich Kiesler published under the name of Frederick Kiesler.

Impressum
Imprint

Österreichische Friedrich und Lillian Kiesler-Privatstiftung, Wien
Austrian Frederick and Lillian Kiesler Private Foundation, Vienna

Wittmann Möbelwerkstätten GmbH

Herausgeber Editors	Monika Pessler, Harald Krejci
Texte Texts	Tulga Beyerle, Harald Krejci
Redaktion Editing	Monika Pessler, Valentina Sonzogni
Übersetzungen Translations	Richard Watts
Grafische Gestaltung Graphic design	MVD Austria: Michael Rieper, Christine Schmauszer, Georg Skerbisch
Schrift Typeface	Glypha, Bell Gothic
Papier Paper	Exposé 140 g, Munken Lynx 150 g
Gesamtherstellung Printed by	Dr. Cantz'sche Druckerei, Ostfildern-Ruit
Fotos Re-Edition Photographs Re-edition	katsey: Theresa Katona und Barbara Seyr Produktion: Simon Frearson
Umschlagabbildung Cover illustration	Friedrich Kiesler, New York, ca. 1950, Foto photograph by Gjon Mili.
Reproduktionen Reproductions	© 2005 für die abgebildeten Werke, falls nicht anders angegeben: Österreichische Friedrich und Lillian Kiesler-Privatstiftung, Wien © 2005 for the reproduced works if not otherwise indicated: Austrian Frederick and Lillian Kiesler Private Foundation, Vienna

Liste der durch Copyright geschützten Objekte und Reproduktionen.
Fehlerhafte oder fehlende Angaben werden in folgenden Auflagen
berücksichtigt. List of art works and photographs protected by copyright.
Errors or omissions will be corrected in subsequent editions.

Abb. Fig. 8 © 2005 André Groult, VG Bild-Kunst, Bonn
Abb. Fig. 9 © 2005 Le Corbusier, FLC/VG Bild-Kunst, Bonn
Abb. Fig. 21 © 2005 Ludwig Mies van der Rohe, VG Bild-Kunst, Bonn
Abb. Fig. 31 © Mervin Beyer, New York
Abb. Fig. 73, 82 © Solomon R.Guggenheim Foundation, New York
Abb. Fig. 94 © Collection Ron Warren and Joshua Mack, New York
Abb. Fig. 95 © 2005 Museum of Modern Art, New York, Scala Florence
Abb. Fig. 107 © Collection Barbara Pine, New York
Abb. Fig. 116 © MMK-Museum für Moderne Kunst Frankfurt am Main
Abb. Fig. 73, 74, 82, 87, 90 © Berenice Abbott, Commerce Graphics Ltd.
Abb. Fig. 17, 18 © Ruth Bernhard
Abb. Fig. 25, 26, 27 © Fay S. Lincoln Inc.
Abb. Fig. 48, 50, 64 © Collection Evan Janis, New York
Abb. Fig. 110 © Ben Schnall
Abb. Fig. 114 © Marsel Loermans
Abb. Fig. 115 © Patrick Gries
Abb. Seite Fig. page 118 © Wittmann Möbelwerkstätten GmbH,
Foto Photograph by Bernhard Angerer
Abb. Seite Fig. pages 106-118 © Österreichische Friedrich und Lillian
Kiesler-Privatstiftung, Wien und Wittmann Möbelwerkstätten GmbH,
Fotos Photograph by katsey

Dank an Thanks to	Ute Barba, Chiara Barbieri, Mervin Beyer, Gertraud Bogner, Maryette Charlton, Catherine Dressler, Karin Denk, Anja Eßlinger, Jane Gamble, Ewald Gruber, Rene Hentschke, Achim Hochdörfer, Ulrike Wittmann, Jürgen Hörth, Evan Janis, Mario Kramer, Annette Kulenkampff, Heike Maier, Jason McCoy, Christine Müller, Stefan Parth, Len Pitkowsky, Don Quaintance, Chiara Riccardi, Philip Rylands, John Shore, Thomas Trummer, Ron Warren, Elisabeth Willhelm, Xenia Wörle

Erschienen im Published by   Hatje Cantz Verlag
Senefelderstraße 12
73760 Ostfildern-Ruit
Deutschland Germany
Tel. +49 711 44050
Fax +49 711 4405220
www.hatjecantz.com

Hatje Cantz books are available internationally at selected
bookstores and from the following distribution partners:

USA/North America – D.A.P., Distributed Art Publishers, New York
www.artbook.com

UK – Art Books International, London, sales@art-bks.com

Australia – Towerbooks, French Forest (Sydney), towerbks@zipworld.com.au

France – Interart, Paris, commercial@interart.fr

Belgium – Exhibitions International, Leuven, www.exhibitionsinternational.be

Switzerland – Scheidegger, Affoltern am Albis, scheidegger@ava.ch

For Asia, Japan, South America, and Africa, as well as for general
questions, please contact Hatje Cantz directly at sales@hatjecantz.de, or visit
our homepage www.hatjecantz.com for further information.

ISBN 3-7757-1544-4
Printed in Germany

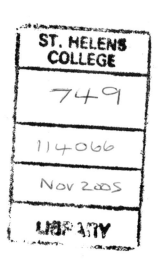

ST. HELENS
COLLEGE

749

114066

Nov 2005

LIBRARY